I have known Scott Glabb for over a decade and have seen him mentor and lead 'challenged students' to dream and reach goals most thought were beyond their reach. In his book, the reader discovers how Scott believed in boys living against all odds and transformed them into winners.

—Lou Correa, California State Senator, Thirty-Fourth District

Inspiring. Heartfelt. Triumphant. After reading this book and how Scott affected these kids' lives, it made me want to drop everything and coach.

—Dan Clark aka "Nitro" of *American Gladiators*

Scott Glabb takes the reader on a poignant journey into the lives and hardships of many of Santa Ana High School's forgotten youth. With unwavering courage, personal sacrifice, and determination, he is able to reach seemingly unreachable kids. Using wrestling as his vehicle for change, he provides tough love to teach these kids that they not only matter, they can also find their place in the world and achieve their dreams.

—Frank Jasper, Dipl. Ac., L.Ac. (Brian Shute in the 1984 film *Vision Quest*)

Glabb gave me confidence, He got my head straight. In *A Saint in the City*, one reads about kids most coaches would give up on, that I would give up on, but Glabb never gave up on them.

—Gilbert Melendez
Mixed Martial Arts Professional Fighter w/ Strikeforce (Santa Ana Wrestling Alumni)

12-31-09

Troy & Jennifer

Many Thanks for looking out and taking care of my mom during your pool events

Many Blessings to you and your family.

A SAINT IN THE CITY

With much appreciation

Scott Gleb[illegible]

Jeremiah 29:11

A SAINT IN THE CITY

coaching at-risk kids to be champions

SCOTT GLABB

with John Scott Lewinski

TATE PUBLISHING & *Enterprises*

A Saint in the City

Published by Tate Publishing & Enterprises, LLC
127 E. Trade Center Terrace | Mustang, Oklahoma 73064 USA
1.888.361.9473 | www.tatepublishing.com

Tate Publishing is committed to excellence in the publishing industry. The company reflects the philosophy established by the founders, based on Psalm 68:11,
"The Lord gave the word and great was the company of those who published it."

Cover design by Lance Waldrop
Interior design by Nathan Harmony

Published in the United States of America

ISBN: 978-1-9332906-1-4
1. Biography & Autobiography: Sports: Wrestling
2. Sports & Recreation: Coaching: Wrestling
09.10.06

NOTE TO READER

All the stories and characters are from my experiences while teaching and coaching at Santa Ana High School in Santa Ana, California. Nothing has been sugarcoated, embellished, or exaggerated.

One might believe, after reading the first few chapters, that the city of Santa Ana and the school are the stereotypical inner-city dwellings embroiled with gangs, poverty, crime, and undocumented immigrants. Unfortunately, when I first arrived there in the late 1980s, it was all of the above. However, over the last two decades, Santa Ana has changed, thankfully, for the better, while still remaining rich with tradition and pride.

The school itself has had a facelift, making it free of graffiti and cleaner than most middle-class high schools I have visited. Moreover, it has since been recognized as one of the safest schools in the district, with a strict dress code and discipline policy. A continued presence of security, administrators, and teachers keep the student body in check and accountable. Architecturally, it is one of the most beautiful buildings in the county as well as and one of the oldest. It is, in my opinion, one of the best-kept secrets in Orange County.

Santa Ana now boasts of its drop in crime and its increase in new homes and businesses; hence, my rationale for writing this book is to share with every athlete, parent, coach, educator, and (anyone else willing to hear the story) how a group of teenagers overcame their inner struggles and outside adversities to rise up and become a success. Including how *one* coach shared with those young men the triumphs and heartaches of growing up.

The intention is certainly not to place the school or the city in a bad light or cause those on the outside anxious about visiting Santa Ana. The goal here is to bring to light the struggles that these young men experienced during a specific period. Society is generally blind to what goes on in certain places and cannot appreciate what some of the Latinos of Santa Ana have to fight for to live a decent life like most of us.

I have grown to love Santa Ana and have been loyal to the school, the streets, the buildings, and its people for over two decades. This is my story about a city that, along with the wrestlers I coached, has changed for the better. As you read of the struggles and adversities some of the wrestlers faced, a parallel can be drawn with the municipality. As each athlete overcame and stood victorious, the metamorphosis of the city was also unfolding alongside each of them, proud of the positive changes made.

A city, a school, and a team of wrestlers all on the same path, a path improved in the quality of life known as the American dream.

DEDICATION

I dedicate this book to all those who encouraged me to write it. I knew I had a story to tell but didn't think anyone would be interested in hearing it. Several individuals, like my physician, Dr. Mitch Watanabe, and fellow teacher Daryl Killion, often told me, "You should write a book about your coaching experience." It took a lot of poking and prodding before I finally got the confidence to do it. Thanks to those who believed in me and knew I could accomplish it. This dedication is also in order to all those Santa Ana wrestlers whom I coached. Without them challenging me, testing me, hurting me, and loving me, I wouldn't have a story.

I learned from my former wrestlers to forgive, to persevere, to be courageous, to be compassionate, to endure, to live for the moment, to laugh at myself, to count my blessings, and to believe that what seems impossible can actually be accomplished. Essentially, they showed me that dreams could come true.

ACKNOWLEDGMENTS

It is important for me to acknowledge all those who helped me during my coaching career. I'd like to thank the people who gave me a helping hand. Without them, my experience and success as a coach would still be a dream.

I want to thank some of the former staff and administrators at Santa Ana High School: my first principal, Lewis Bratcher, and athletic director, Bill Ross. They had confidence in me to hire me as a teacher and coach. I can't forget my previous athletic director, Frank Alvarado, who made me feel important and valued me. He is a man who really respects the sport of wrestling as well as Principal Dan Salcedo, whose constant pats on the back and words of affirmation helped me to press on. I must mention Al Mijares, Santa Ana Unified School District's former superintendent, for sending me notes of encouragement and appreciation from time to time, as well as our current superintendent Jane Russo, who understands the importance of sports programs in our schools. Then there are my old high school coaches, Charlie Lemcke, Norm Friehauf, and Pat King. They showed me what it meant to have backbone and how to coach with intensity. Their love for the sport inspired me to be a coach. My appreciation also goes out to all the past and present assistant coaches I've worked with: Alex Becerra, Tim Byers, Luis De La Rosa, Tony Gomez, Froilan Gonzalez, Joe Gonzales, Bill Haley, Chuck Hinman, Tom Hutchinson, Rudy Justo, Jerry Laforteza, Rick Lara, José Leon, Sadie Morales, José Morales, José Najera, Ron Orellana, Jaime Orendain, Mat Orndorff, Tony Perez, Sam Pina, Mark Senesac, Fernado Serratos, Juan Serna, Luis Ramirez, and Vince Silva, as well as all the Santa Ana wrestling alumni who stepped into that practice room and on to the mat. Those men unconditionally took the time to coach, counsel, lead, and inspire all those who participated in the program. Other coaches who have contributed to the success of the program are Terry Young, Joe Rousell, Mario Lara, and Bob Glassman. All four are PE teachers at the local intermediate schools, and they took the time to include the sport of wrestling in their physical education curriculum. I will not forget the generosity of Coach Steve Stewart, who allowed my wrestlers to attend his weekly camps and clinics at no cost. I would also like to recognize some of the wrestlers' parents who have continued to help the program even after their sons have graduated. I could always count on Gilbert Melendez, Dave Carbajal (Mr. C), the late Larry Lopez, and the Cano Family to help out with fundraising and working the concession stand at home meets and tournaments. I appreciate Marshall and Julianne Howard's emotional, financial, and, most importantly, academic support of the wrestlers as well as the Valencia family, who has given thousands of dollars in scholarship money to the school and our wrestling program. Both families have shown a genuine care and concern for the overall well-being of many wrestlers on the team. I am also grateful to José Garcia, Gil Guiterrez, and Esther Guiterrez for starting the kids' age group wrestling program, "the Santa Ana Wolfpack." A few years ago, they made a sincere commitment to begin a neighborhood-wrestling club for kids five to thirteen years of age. Their success with the program parallels that of the Santa Ana High School's wrestling team. I am proud of them and respect their dedication to further the sport of wrestling. I need to recognize the most important male role model in my life, Michael Miller. He led me to the Lord when I was thirteen years old. Since then, he has been my mentor, my counselor, my pastor, and my best friend. I love you, Mike. Special thanks to John Scott Lewinski for helping me write this book and Cherry-Ann Carew for the time she took to help edit this book in the beginning stages.

Blessings go to my mother, Lou, who raised my sister and me in a single-parent home, earned minimum wage her entire life, yet always found a way to give us what we needed to be successful.

Appreciation to my sister, Louette, who took me in and gave me a place to live when I first moved to California. She walked with me during the darkest times of my depression and prayed for me daily. Then there is my dad, Larry. Though he wasn't available emotionally and didn't spend much time with me while growing up, it's important for me to hear him now say, "I'm proud of you, Son, and what you've done with your team."

Special thanks to First Baptist Church of Santa Ana, Donnie Dee and Mark Boyer of the Southern California Fellowship of Christian Athletes (FCA) staff as well as Pastors Adam Ayers and Mike Perkinson of Disciple's Church in Costa Mesa. These ministries continually supported me and kept my team in prayer. They recognized the difficult task I had teaching, coaching, and ministering to these kids year round and encouraged me when I was down. I could never forget José Campo, coach at Mt. Carmel High School in San Diego and one of my few close friends in the sport of wrestling. He has faithfully directed the FCA Wrestling Camp for the past fifteen years and has been like a second coach to all my wrestlers who have attended camp with him. He sincerely cares about the wrestlers from Santa Ana. He is an inspiration to all who know him. A great deal of gratitude goes to

Bill Farrington of the Asics Corporation. He and the company have been fantastic about donating shoes and equipment to kids from our program in need. They make it a point to invest in the community and give back to the sport of wrestling. I also need to extend my gratefulness to several doctors in the community who have served many of the wrestlers medical needs without charge. They are Mitch Watanabe MD, Ken Thaler MD, Michael Glandorf DC, Donald Apodaca OD, Dr. Adams, and Mark Gomez.

I must also recognize some community leaders who believed in my purpose and mission at Santa Ana High School and for the last decade were always there to give me a helping hand and support the wrestling program: All past and present Santa Ana Unified School District board members along with John Palacios and former board member Rosie Avila, California State Senator Lou Correa, and Santa Ana City Council members Michele Martinez and Sal Tinajero.

And finally, and most importantly, I thank my wife, Andrea. She never stopped believing in me. She knew coaching was my calling and passion, and she never set demands on me to be home early or skip a practice or tournament to be with her. Her enduring love and patience toward me demands my appreciation of her. She is the wife every coach needs and deserves.

TABLE OF CONTENTS

FOREWORD

When a friend asked me to read a magazine article about a high school coach, little did I know how my life would change. The article told the story how this coach poured his entire life into the members of his wrestling team. The high school he coached was similar to the one I was raised in. The students were from low income areas, and their team meant the world to them. I wanted to meet the man who treated his athletes like his sons, putting their development as his top priority.

As luck would have it, I found myself sitting next to Scott Glabb the very next weekend. I introduced myself and have been amazed the more I learn about this loving, caring man. In an age of selfishness and winning at all cost, Scott has proven that good planning and hard work is still the best way to achieve success. He has raised thousands of dollars to enable his kids the chance to travel, compete, find jobs, and continue their education. Many times Scott's hard work went without much thanks. But our loving God knows his intentions and has rewarded Scott with a beautiful wife and two loving sons.

It has always been my belief that God will reward you with the desires of your heart if you work extremely hard and make the right lifestyle choices. Scott is the perfect example. We all can learn from the pride of Santa Ana Wrestling.

—José Campo
Coach Mt. Carmel High School
San Diego, California
USA Wrestling Magazine
National Coach of the Year

INTRODUCTION

As I continue to coach Santa Ana High School wrestlers, I often remind myself none of them should have been there. Certainly not me. I was supposed to be happily married and coaching a nationally ranked wrestling program back in the suburbs of Seattle, not living in bachelor hell and babysitting a ragtag team in a Southern California barrio so filled with gunfire parents forbade their kids to walk home from school.

Certainly not Tony "the Bean" Perez; he was not a candidate to make it through his Southern California tournaments, much less an odds-on favorite to become a finalist at the California State Wrestling Championships. How could he now find himself in the final match of his weight class at the High School National Championships? It was all a dream—an American dream.

To most of us the American dream today is no more than a hack politician's slickly scripted but strangely indigestible sound bite stolen from long-petrified textbooks. It is easy for us to forget what we never knew, how hard fought every step still is for each new generation.

This dream shows how a lost man from the Pacific Northwest, never realizing he was actually looking for himself, found a generation of equally lost kids and how they each found inner strength to fight day after day—both on the wrestling mat and outside the protective walls of the wrestling room, while all those around kept telling them they did not belong.

It is a dream about the courage to try to make something of ourselves as individuals and Americans. It is a dream of Tony standing on the mat in the ring that last time and staring down a seemingly impossible opportunity.

How did he manage to come across his last opponent? The obstacle to his young life's greatest possible achievement: a slab of solitary muscle standing before him; a wrestler with fifty-three straight wins and no losses. A wrestler long expected to seize the national high school title without serious effort.

Long before facing his opponent, Tony had no business anywhere *near* a wrestling mat. He was supposed to quit wrestling when he was told to give up the sport to help feed his five brothers and sisters. He certainly should have walked off the mat when his parents refused to sign the permission slip to allow him to continue wrestling, much less offer him support, encouragement, or approval. Tony rose out of a sea of total opposition.

Among the tens of thousands of fiercely competitive high school wrestlers spending countless hours endlessly drilling in sweat-drenched wrestling rooms in all fifty states, how could Tony be the last one still standing in the championship match for his weight class with the only unbeaten wrestler in the country?

How many of his teammates back home in school dreamed of similar success? How many spent their spare hours in the self-inflicted torture of a wrestling room, molding still immature minds, muscles, and characters on often blood-splattered mats? Surely not the one whose parents offered him the holy grail of young manhood—the keys to a new car—if he would quit wrestling, or the teammate whose gangbanger buddies patiently awaited his return outside the wrestling room, or the one who was jumped and robbed at gunpoint on his way home from practice when he stayed that extra hour.

For them, it was over. Thousands of moments individually make up each of our daily lives: in the mere seconds when bad advice is followed or in that moment of weakness when temptation wins. This day could have been denied for Tony.

Each of the wrestlers could yet stumble and fall, naturally fulfilling society's unnatural expectations of gang life, prepping juvenile hall, and matriculating to prison or at best becoming high school dropouts groomed for minimum wage jobs and barely supported illegitimate children. Maybe they could graduate from high school; then if everything aligned perfectly, attending the local community college was, at best, a distant dream.

Young immigrants from Mexico and El Salvador crammed into struggling schools in a densely populated city had little hope for the future. Their families and culture had other plans for them. They were to be shepherded into foregoing their dreams once they grew strong enough for man's work—work that would help to support a stream of siblings. Time did not matter: a year, a month, a week, or even a day. What difference did the moment make when they knew they would never be anywhere but where they already were? Not Tony. He had a chance at glory and history.

Three time periods, two minutes in length—the time for an egg to boil—that determines a national high school wrestling champion. In an alien place, thousands of miles from anything Tony knew, he faced six minutes of mat time in suburban Pennsylvania to determine the rest of his life. He was competing athletically on a national level. He could win. He could graduate high school with honors. He could earn a scholarship to an academically challenging university. He could build a future with a job, not all because of a wrestling match, but because that match could teach him to believe in possibilities even when none of this was supposed to happen. Nevertheless, it did happen to the kids I coached and the ones I still coach today.

WELCOME TO SANTA ANA

1990

We know what we are, but know not what we may become.
—William Shakespeare, English poet and playwright

Seventy-two to zero. That was not a score. It was a massacre: Christians fed to lions, Reagan over Mondale, Custer at Little Bighorn. It seemed like more than mere cross-town wrestling rivals facing off in a hot Orange County, California gym.

As I sat on the bench, watching the slaughter through the cracks of my fingers, I knew it was a long, difficult road ahead. The humiliation that ran through my body, coupled with embarrassment, told me that the coaching gig at Santa Ana High School would prove much more challenging than I expected.

After the match, a lone fan from the crowd consoled me, "You can always look on the bright side; you could have lost seventy-eight to zero."

That is the highest possible margin of defeat in a dual meet with thirteen weight classes competing. I felt that the score was a reflection on how the whole season was going so far, doomed and hopeless. And if the score wasn't a sign of my destiny, then watching my heavyweight chase his opponent with a folding chair after he lost, was. He never caught his nemesis; therefore, he just threw the chair across the mat toward the other team's bench. That was the last match my heavyweight ever wrestled. Frustrated, I wondered what was in store for the Saints of Santa Ana. Santa Ana High School was built in 1889 and is the oldest high school in Orange County. The mascot for Santa Ana High School is the Saints. They were called the Owls before 1925. For some unknown reason, the name Saints was used in the school newspaper in May of 1925; the mascot name stuck and is still used today.

In the years before I found myself in Santa Ana, I always disliked going to Southern California to visit my younger sister who lived in Long Beach and worked as an airline ticket agent. During summers, I headed down from my home state of Washington to spend some time with her. What I hated most about Southern California were the plastic people running around and the constant pressure to appear good-looking and successful.

After several visits, I decided California would be the last place in the world I would like to live. However, I can thank an old girlfriend, Diana, who was my sister's best friend from high school, for bringing me south. After a year and a half of a long-distance relationship and getting turned down by my old high school for a coaching and teaching position, Diana asked, "What do you have to lose?" and finally convinced me to move down to the place I dreaded the most.

It was the most difficult decision I have ever had to make. I had a nice little comfort zone going in Vancouver, Washington, with my friends, my family, my church, and everything familiar. In spite of this, I could not land a full-time teaching and coaching position in my hometown.

I was also in the midst of battling my way out of a deep psychological depression. After graduating from college, I found myself slowly slipping into a state of severe depression. In fact, I was suicidal. At first it was hard to pinpoint the cause of my depression. However, after many years of counseling and a look back at my bittersweet childhood, I found the origin. The best part of my childhood was growing up in Washington. I lived in a small home on an acre-and-a-half of property. Living on that much land, with acres and acres of fields all around, allowed us to grow up much differently than the kids I coach. I had a tree fort that we often used for sleepovers, and I had BB gun fights with my neighborhood friends. I owned two mini-bikes that I rode for miles throughout the woods and fields that surrounded my house. I have endless memories of riding my bike to China Ditch (a small creek,) catching frogs and crawdads, jumping off bridges into rivers, swinging on ropes into lakes, playing baseball, and just spending time with friends. I feel lucky to have had such an active childhood, but it did not go without moments of confusion, instability, and disorder. I had a father whose continued drinking became a problem for us all. You couldn't ask for a better father when he wasn't pounding them down. He was the one who built me my tree forts and bought my mini-bikes. He took us on camping trips that seemed to be almost weekly. He was a true outdoorsman who taught me how to hunt and fish before I knew what the terms even meant. But by age seven, that all ended. I started to see the rage alcohol brought out in my dad. When he drank, he became a different man, a man I feared, and it became impossible to have a normal father-son relationship with my dad. My mom did the sensible thing and got a divorce from my father. It wasn't long before he got remarried to a woman who had two sons of her own. I no longer felt I was the apple of his eye.

At first, I believed I was depressed because of some self-image issues. I didn't like the way I looked. But as I later understood,

I manifested my internal painful relationship with my father into something I could see ... myself. Soon, I became obsessed with these issues. I decided there was no way to change what I hated about myself, so I lost hope. There is one thing I learned through my depression: *when one loses hope, one loses the future.* When one has no future, thoughts of suicide are entertained. When I saw life as hopeless, my dream of being a teacher and coach dissipated, and thoughts of suicide began to haunt me on a daily basis. Luckily, I never attempted the deadly act; however, I did think through several plans of how I would do it if I ever did get the guts to take my own life. I believe it was my fear of eternal damnation that always stopped me short.

I became a born-again Christian at thirteen years old and had a strong faith in God. However, my faith began to waver as the depression grew worse. Finally, a friend of mine, Michael Miller, my high school youth pastor, convinced me to check myself into a psychiatric care unit. Within the first couple of hours of my stay, I realized that most of the other patients were more than just depressed. There were patients with schizophrenia, multiple-personality disorder, and dementia, to name a few. I didn't belong there. I was depressed but not out of my mind. So I had to make a decision—kill myself when I got out of there or find a way to overcome and beat this depression. During my stay, I met with a psychiatrist who diagnosed me with obsessive-compulsive disorder and put me on some antidepressants. I was released from the hospital a few days later and immediately signed up for welfare because I was still too depressed to work. I thought to myself, *How did my life wind up in such a mess?* On welfare, jobless, depressed, and confused, I decided I really had absolutely nothing to lose and left behind the quiet and comfortable life and moved to the comparable chaos of Southern California.

Luckily, my sister Louette was living in Huntington Beach, California, so I had a place to lay my head until I could find a job and get back on my feet. I started attending Disciple's Church in Costa Mesa with my girlfriend, which was where I met Pastor Mike Perkinson. He offered to help me understand why I was depressed. At this point, I was desperate for help and just wanted to get some fragment of my life back from the way it was. I had already gone through several therapists and counselors, walking out on all of them because I didn't think they could help me. Therefore, I made a commitment to meet with Mike on a weekly basis, in hopes that he could help me battle my way out of this funk I was in.

I spent my days looking for a job, riding a bike to the beach, and just moping around, feeling sorry for myself. I figured I would not be able to get a teaching job at the high school level anyway since I did not have a California teaching credential. California had some strict requirements to become a teacher, and my Washington State teaching credential didn't meet their standards. Finding alternative work was not easy either. Hard up for a buck, I resorted to selling snow cones at local supermarkets. Years ago, Michael Miller had bought a snow cone machine for us to do fundraising in Vancouver. Now, the same kind of machine was a main source of my income.

After my travels and the courage it took to head to California, I found myself standing in a parking lot at the local grocery store, praying that people would pay one dollar to cool down from the heat. The homeless guy cleaning car windows made off with more money in two hours than I made in a day. I even gave him a buck to clean my truck windows and a free cone because I felt sorry for him. I had a Washington State teaching credential, a BA in education, and a BA in communication studies—all this education to end up pushing a cup of crushed ice and flavored syrup. Utterly humiliated, my self-esteem was never lower.

In due course, I landed a job interview with McDonnell Douglas, the airplane manufacturer, for a position as a corporate trainer, a career track that somewhat interested me. The pay was more than adequate. However, luck had it that Marina High School in upscale Huntington Beach, had an opening for a head wrestling coach. My aspiration since I was sixteen years old was to be a teacher and head wrestling coach. Why not talk to the athletic director at Marina High?

Our meeting went well, and after background and reference checks, the athletic director offered me the coaching job. I would also serve as a resident substitute teacher, reporting to the school every day to cover absent teachers. To be fully credentialed, I needed to pass the CBEST (California Basic Education Standardized Test) and pick up thirty credits in English. Not only did I need a BA in English, I also had to take more classes to qualify for the state credential. To stay in California meant more school, something I had no more enthusiasm to pursue. Besides, I figured I would be going back to Washington soon anyway. More college courses were out of the question. Luckily, I was able to apply for a California state emergency teaching credential. Being a resident sub was not a bad deal. Little preparation was involved, and that allowed more time to focus on coaching, a skill that I soon realized took much more work than I anticipated.

I spent two years as the head wrestling coach at Marina. It was difficult to fill the shoes of Paul LeBlanc, my predecessor, whom everyone loved and respected. I was young, inexperienced, and depressed. Those factors combined to make my short stay difficult. I was not used to coaching kids who wore a bit of arrogance and self-centeredness on their sleeves. To be honest, I am not sure whom I was used to coaching since this was my first job as a head coach. I butted heads with most of the kids and made several mistakes and poor decisions. Parents were supportive, but they also tended to keep me in check.

At the end of year two, I was ready to move on, as I was not happy within myself, but I was never one to run from hard times. I could not endure the fog of disrespect I encountered every day and the lack of commitment the wrestlers had to the sport that I loved. I also realize now, as I look back, that many of the mistakes and poor decisions I made as a coach stemmed from my continued struggle with depression. I was too sensitive to some of the wrestlers' lack of commitment, and I was very self-centered. I found that my depression made me a very selfish person. I did what I wanted to do when I wanted to do it no matter who it hurt or put out. I was getting too caught up in trying to make myself feel good, thinking that winning would be my antidepressant. I guess I was hoping it would relieve me of my feelings of despair. It did not. However, after two years of counseling with Mike Perkinson, I was making progress. He had me reading recovery books that helped me comprehend the dynamics of a dysfunctional family and understand what codependency was and how it related to my life. He gave me projects to do and papers to write. I diligently did everything he asked of me. And then, finally, we got to the real issue. It had nothing to do with my poor self-image and the way I looked. It all came down to my unbalanced, absent relationship with my father. (That's when it hit me—the root cause.) I finally had to acknowledge that all I wanted was to have him play catch with me, show me how to change the oil in my car, or be in my corner, cheering for me at my sporting events. It all made sense now. For years, I resented my dad for the way he abandoned me. I basically manifested the internal pain of my jacked-up relationship with my dad into something physical, something I could see in the mirror every day and complain about. In time, I admitted that I needed him, forgave him for the pain he caused me, and slowly tried to move on with my life. The counseling, medication, support from my sister and mother, and especially from coaching wrestling all aided in my healing process.

Consequently, I resigned from my job at Marina. It was clear it was not working out. The unhappiness between myself and the wrestlers was mutual. The regrettable situation left me without a job again and without a connection to the sport that guided so much of my life.

I grew up in a single parent, low-income household and lived in a neighborhood where the kids were more interested in smoking pot than playing sports. Little did I know that going out for wrestling in seventh grade would change my life. Wrestling improved my self-esteem and gave me the confidence I needed to say no to the peer pressure of doing drugs and alcohol. It gave me a sense of belonging; I had a group on campus that I could identify with, something for which all teenagers yearn. Wrestling taught me perseverance. So many times, I felt like giving up on school, work, and relationships, but knew I had to press on to make them work. I learned what it means to be committed to something, to follow through, to be dependable, to make my yes be yes and my no be no. During my junior year in high school, I firmly decided that if I wanted to stay linked to the sport I knew I would have to become a high school teacher and coach. That meant a college education. It scares me to think where I would be today if I had never wrestled.

Those factors combined into a sense of desperation that led me to apply for the wrestling coach position at Santa Ana High School—a job that I applied for only because, apparently, the other coaches out there knew something I did not. Perhaps they knew the team had the potential to lose a meet seventy-two to zero.

The high school sits in the middle of Santa Ana, California. It is a city nestled in beautiful Orange County. Unfortunately, it once ranked number one in the nation among large cities in urban hardship, according to the Nelson A. Rockefeller Institute. Its ranking is based on income, education, and housing conditions. For instance, 56 percent of those twenty-five and older who reside in Santa Ana have no high school diploma. Furthermore, the population of Santa Ana has doubled in the last few years, causing a housing shortage. Some students are now forced to live in three-bedroom tract homes or two-bedroom apartments crammed with relatives and strangers-turned-roommates.

They survive ten to twenty people under one roof, adhering to a strict schedule of when to use the bathroom and the kitchen. These statistics alone should have served as a warning that I was in over my head. I was curious however, as to why the athletic director, Bill Ross, hired me on the spot when I applied.

"You're hired!" he said.

"But you haven't asked me any questions yet," I replied, surprised.

"That's because you are the only one who has applied for the job. Welcome to Santa Ana."

Ross said he would also find me a teaching position, and with joyful hesitation, I accepted the post. Thus began the most demanding and painstaking job I have ever endured. It did not take long for me to have second thoughts, since I admit that I did not even like driving through Santa Ana, let alone teaching there; but, something led me to that pariah of a wrestling team. Call it God's timing, fate, or chance, but I believe I was placed with that team and those kids for a reason.

Also, with the growth I was making in my therapy I needed to use what little self-esteem I was gaining to mold a young bunch of hooligans into a group of athletes who never once dreamed of becoming champions in the sport of wrestling; and further, I could not understand why most of the students even came out for the sport.

I came from the old-school command style approach of coaching: I call the shots, you do what I say and don't question me. I always stressed dedication, discipline, commitment, and hard work for success as an athlete. These words were light years away from my team's vocabulary.

I finally concluded that they did not wrestle for the same reasons I did. Some were wrestling because my assistant coaches,

Bill Haley and Chuck Hinman, (also the sophomore football coaches) told their players that they had no choice but to try wrestling for two weeks. They were given the option to quit if it was not their cup of tea. Others on the wrestling team were athletes dropped from a sixth-period athletics class and needed a place to hang out and waste time until the semester ended. Some were there because their friends were wrestling, and the rest who came were just looking for a place to fit in or something to be a part of so they could gain a sense of belonging and direction.

As I worked with them over the months, the wrestling room became a haven. A place that attracted the lost and lonely on campus, the talentless and clumsy, as well as the corrupt, the angry, and the misguided. In fact, wrestling their opponents was effortless compared to the real matches they faced off the mat. These boys wrestled against some adversities beyond the belief of anyone who never lived as they did. The same hardship, misfortune, and pain plagued these boys today as much as they did when I first started coaching; only now the aggrieved wear a different face. The real challenge I had with these boys wasn't trying to get them to win but trying to get them to break the cycle of dysfunction they lived under, solve the daily problems they were burdened with, and convince them to turn their life around for the better. I soon realized I needed these boys as much as they needed me. Helping them fix their problems in turn helped me to fix mine. Coaching this team inspired me to discover my purpose and restart my life from the pain of my depression.

Now, I look back to the first day I walked into the wrestling room and wonder how God ever managed to use a broken man, like myself, to build the program into a winner and the team into a source of salvation for the wrestlers. I wondered too how I guided a deflated wrestling program into one of the finer teams in the state of California. More importantly than my coaching success, I wondered how the *boys* beat the odds. How did they rise up out of their oppressed situations to graduate from high school, wrestle in college, and find careers that pay more than the coach who saw little hope for them? Many high school coaches shine with pride and pat themselves on the back for their success in landing their athletes scholarships and sending them to Division I colleges.

However, for *this* coach, I was just delighted that these depraved, broken, and ill-fated boys rose above the city's clutches and made their dreams, as well as mine, become a reality.

RONNIE ORTEGA-ENANO

1990–1993

Life is an adventure in forgiveness.

—Norman Cousins,
prominent political journalist and author

I first met Ronnie when his football coach decided to have his sophomore team try out for wrestling. I was a first-year coach and needed as many wrestlers as I could get. The sophomore football coach wanted all the kids on the team to try the sport for two weeks; then any who did not like it could quit.

Ronnie was one of those kids that joined after football season. Although he only stood five feet one inch, he had the perfect body frame of a lightweight wrestler. He had short, wavy hair and a contagious smile that was seldom seen. Unfortunately, what *was* seen was the chip on his shoulder and the attitude he carried along with it. He was not Mexican but Puerto Rican, a difference

I found hard to distinguish. He later earned the unpleasant nickname Enano (which means midget in Spanish) because he was shorter than most of the other boys on the team.

He had a hard exterior and a lot of talent that he did not know he possessed. He was born to wrestle. He also had a problems being committed and staying disciplined to both the sport and school. Ronnie always tried to get out of practice by using feeble excuses such as, "I need to go home and wash the dishes." He had a lot of anger in him. It seemed like every Monday he'd come to school with black eyes, fat lips, and bruises. He had been fighting. When asked what happened, his reasoning was that someone disrespected his mother or kids were picking on him about his height. Whatever it was, he did not have a lot of patience, and he exploded when confronted.

He was not the type who appeared to be in trouble, but he often *found* trouble because he dealt with his problem emotionally. He struggled to maintain the 2.0 grade point average necessary to compete. However, I could see there was more to him than met the eye; aside from so much internal rage, I felt he could do well in school if he applied himself. He became one of the many wrestlers on the team who challenged me and kept me on my toes. I invested a lot of time trying to make changes in his life that he would find positive. I wanted to encourage him to live a better lifestyle.

After I came to know him, I found that in seventh grade Ronnie was convicted of grand theft auto. He stole a car as a juvenile and did some community service. I learned that there were many crimes committed, including a credit card scheme with a friend.

Ronnie was offered a summer job at a hospital through a Red Cross program at the high school. The position gave him access to the database of people who recently passed away. He knew what their illnesses were, what prescriptions they took, etc. He took their information and sold them to a man who lived in his apartment complex. However, Ronnie knew he was up to something, and soon he began to withhold the information until the man included him. Soon he was a part of an illegal operation. In short, they used the dead person's data to fill out credit card applications, rent an apartment, hook up a phone line with an answering machine, and make sure the phone was manned when the credit card companies called. I was amazed to learn he was capable of concocting such illegal acts.

Ronnie boasted that he could steal a car anytime because he knew how to disarm car alarms. He stole batteries, hubcaps, you name it—he stole it at one time or another before he got into high school. He was a thug and a thief, living the wrong lifestyle and hanging out with the wrong people. Strangely enough, it showed what he *could* accomplish if he set his mind to something, but I wanted him to channel his energies into more positive things.

Ronnie had a couple of brothers, but it did not appear as if they had much influence on him. His father was an alcoholic and was not there for him. He lived with his mother, but home was chaotic and unstable. Ronnie found himself alone on the streets, wandering and looking for something to do.

About midway through that first season, he began to dedicate himself to the sport a little more. Maybe my speeches about commitment and fortitude were starting to take root with him. Although the dedication was not yet what I wanted to see, at least he was in the wrestling room every day, putting forth some effort.

Sure, he still found excuses. One day, he offered a corny pretext to leave. I watched him walk away and did not buy the reason he gave. Something inside told me he would never set foot in the wrestling room again. He was done.

Ronnie did return to the wrestling room a few days later, although over the following weeks his presence was inconsistent. I do not know what it was that kept bringing him back. Maybe wrestling offered him a safe haven. Perhaps it was a place for him to take out all that anger, hurt, and resentment that boiled inside him. I knew he dealt with some ugly things while growing up, and I think he found a sport in which he could release all the pent-up frustration since he was not good at talking about it.

Surprisingly, Ronnie finished his first year of wrestling on the varsity team. . Many first-year wrestlers ended up on varsity. I started the season with thirty of them and finished with about twenty; my biggest struggle was filling a lineup. Yes, he still got into more than his share of trouble, but by the end of that sophomore year, Ronnie was sold on the sport of wrestling. He continued to train all spring and summer to make himself better.

In my second season as coach, when Ronnie was a junior, we had an improved team. Now we were counting on him to lead the team. He won many matches and placed in tournaments as a varsity wrestler at 112 pounds. The time came to wrestle Huntington Beach High School, the defending league champions, and the school that had beaten us the year before by that infamous score of seventy-two to zero.

Huntington's best wrestler also came in at 112 pounds, and Ronnie went out there and wrestled horribly. I could not understand what the problem was. After the season, I found out he had been smoking marijuana before the match and was stoned on the mat. I do not know if he thought it was something that would help him perform better, but it ended up hurting him and the team a great deal, as we lost the meet by six points. Suffice it to say, if Ronnie had won that match, that would have provided the point swing we needed to tie the team that beat us so badly a year earlier.

He felt pretty awful about losing that match, and even worse about his foolish behavior. I was disappointed with him. Then he presented me with another issue at seventeen years old, he had a severe drinking problem. During our spring break practice, he and Johnny Martinez came into the wrestling room one day smelling of alcohol. They said they wanted to wrestle me, perhaps believing that the alcohol would make them tough.

I will never forget that day because my feelings were badly hurt. I had grown very close to both of them. I felt like a father reacting to his sons coming into his house drunk and making challenges. I accepted their challenge and called them on to the mat. As I wrestled one after the other, I used legal wrestling moves to afflict some serious pain and anguish. It was the last time they showed up drunk in front of me.

By his senior year, Ronnie had shaped up to become one of the best wrestlers on the team. With his improved training and competition, he was a great asset to the program. Ronnie was my right-hand man and one of the captains of our team that season. He would often assist in my fundraising efforts to support the program. I was organizing a fireworks stand one summer and looked to Ronnie and some other eighteen-year-old seniors for a helping hand. I received no parental support during the first few years of building the program. Therefore, it was up to me and the wrestlers to raise the funds needed to keep the program afloat.

We had a fireworks stand in one of the toughest neighborhoods in Santa Ana. Our first year working the stand, we were lucky enough to fend off the gangbangers and other criminal elements that hovered around the stand, waiting for the moment to seize what fireworks they could get.

However, we were not so fortunate this time. When we showed up to help unload the delivery truck of fireworks, the drivers mentioned how run down and dirty the strip mall was where the stand was located. They voiced their concern for their safety, noticing some local gangbangers casing the stand. The fireworks stands were left unlocked, until occupied with the fireworks and those manning the stands from the organization selling them. These open stands provide shelter for local transients.

I noticed one of those transients left a little "gift" for us in the stand—piles of human waste. Neither Ronnie nor I had the time or resources to clean up this disgusting mess, and since the drivers needed to unload and move on to their next stop, we decided to set the cases of fireworks next to the stand until we had time to clean up the aforementioned gift.

As we stacked the boxes, a gang surrounded us about thirty feet away. I had some suspicion that they might try to rob us but thought it impossible—surely not in broad daylight. Before my next thought, in the twinkle of an eye, they pounced on the boxes of fireworks like a pack of lions on a gazelle. From all sides they rushed us, grabbed the boxes, and fled.

Without hesitation, I pursued one of them across the street, through his turf, thinking of the program and how our fireworks fundraiser was the main source of income for the team. I was enraged with their bravado and could not believe they would steal from a non-profit group.

However, as I raced down the street I suddenly came to my senses and realized where I was. I slowed and watched the thugs speed off with our profits. My life was not worth a box or two of Piccolo Petes and Flashing Fountains. I returned to the stand and told the drivers to load up what was left after the raid.

"Let's go," I said to Ronnie.

"You are right, Coach. They'll be back for more anyway and will harass us all week when we work the stand."

He would know—he grew up on those cruel and unforgiving streets. I guess if there was any consolation that came from our decision to abandon the fireworks stand was the fact that we never had to clean up those piles of crap.

Santa Ana is an area that caters to the Hispanic culture, especially immigrants who do not speak English. Any time Fourth Street is mentioned, the wrestlers laugh because it is considered a joke. It is where all the wild stuff happens in their neighborhood. Ronnie had described times when he and his friends cruised Fourth Street, teasing and mocking the transvestites. I thought that was the limit of contact with the cross dressers. I later found out, however, that they hung out with the transvestites—their new friends—more often than not.

Ronnie and the guys would meet at one location and hang out together because they had no money to eat out or do anything fun. They had a tough time being entertained. Instead of going home to eat and meeting up again later, they would go to the homes of transvestites. There were different stories from each of the boys, but it became clear that more went on there than I cared to hear about. They engaged in strip shows and flirted with the transvestites for food and money. It was an ugly favor-for-favor arrangement. To hear that these young men would sacrifice their dignity and integrity for some food and a little money shocked me to the core.

Fortunately, I got Ronnie and many of the other troubled wrestlers into the Fellowship of Christian Athletes. FCA is a high school campus ministry. I figured there was nothing else I could really do for them except maybe help them find the Lord. I grew up on the wrong side of the tracks, so to speak, in a single-parent home, but I accepted Jesus Christ as my personal Savior when I was thirteen. My family did not have a lot of money and faced a lot of adversity. I believe tackling those challenges got me where I am today and helped me make the decision to turn my life over to God.

I decided we might never win as a team, but maybe I could get these kids back on track in life. They all had a foundation of religion through Catholicism. They had all been baptized and attended Mass, so the seed had been planted. I just tried to foster it. I took them to church and applied for scholarships to send several of them to FCA wrestling camp in the summer.

They made a sincere commitment then, but I knew putting

them back on the streets of Santa Ana would return them to family problems, gangs, school troubles, and a lot of other different pressures they would have to deal with as kids. Soon they started backsliding from their faith, and it became a constant struggle to keep them focused and on course.

Ronnie emerged as a league champion his senior year and graduated. He went on to wrestle at the local junior college, but the outside influences were simply too strong. He lacked the fortitude and perseverance to look ahead and stay away from all the bad things that awaited him.

In the years following his wrestling career, I made Ronnie my assistant at the high school, hoping that the link to the program might help him keep his life together, but he still struggled with drinking and drugs. He was irresponsible, often not showing up to practice when I needed him.

During his time as assistant coach, Ronnie occasionally borrowed my truck to run errands. However, I found out several years later that he was really using it to heist appliances and electronic equipment at a local variety store. His older brother worked as head of security for a retail chain and allowed Ronnie and his friends to take what they wanted as long as he got a piece of the pie.

My vehicle was an *accomplice* in this illegal activity. Though I forgave Ronnie, it was a shock and a real letdown. When I learned what he had done, it hurt to think he lied and took advantage of my generosity. However, I understood how drugs and alcohol could change a man; addiction supersedes relationships.

I became a little hard on him, and we had a classic love/hate relationship. Sometimes, we could not stand each other for what the other did, but we also loved each other for the endurance and commitment we shared. On one occasion, we were standing outside the 7-Eleven near the school when we noticed a local gangbanger, one of the bad guys from Ronnie's apartment complex, on the telephone nearby. He was not a wrestler, but we recognized him as one of the students from Santa Ana High. Suddenly, a truck pulled up, and three other gangbangers jumped out and pulled him off the phone. Two proceeded to beat the living hell out of him before our shocked eyes, while the other kept a look-out, making sure no one would step in to interfere.

I asked myself, *What should I do. Should I step in? Should I help this kid? Does one of them have a gun? What will I be getting involved in if I step into this?*

When the beating was over, the three guys jumped back into their truck and got out of there, leaving their victim in a bloody heap. I regained my composure, feeling horrible that I did not do anything to help. I immediately ran into 7-Eleven and asked for help. No one lifted a finger because they were afraid to get involved. I grabbed some wet paper towels and cleaned the beaten victim up as best I could.

I asked if he wanted me to call the police or file a report on his behalf as I helped him to his home nearby, but he declined. I also asked if he was in a gang, and he denied it, but it was obvious to me; he was wearing the gang attire.

"I feel awful for not stepping in to help," I told Ronnie as he looked at me sideways.

"You know, Glabb, that guy knew what he was getting himself into when he joined a gang. You have got to expect that kind of thing when you become a gangbanger."

That did not offer any comfort, but it sounded like the hard truth. It did not change the fact that I wished I had helped more, even though the kid knew the risks when he signed up for that "team."

I took a good look at Ronnie. He was a tough kid, streetwise, and in his best moments, sincere, kindhearted, and funny. Yet, he had that explosive streak in him that straddled the fine line between good and bad and contributed to all the pain and suffering he experienced and caused for himself over the years.

Ronnie was molested by a family friend when he was seven

years old, and I knew that lit the fuse that led to all the rage and misery he generally walked into. He admitted that his parents knew it was going on but looked the other way. I imagined that nightmare, to be abandoned like that by the people he trusted the most to protect him.

After leaving the wrestling staff, Ronnie fell off the face of the earth. That was disappointing, maybe because I felt a little abandoned by my friend, but he called me a few weeks later from air force boot camp to let me know that he joined the military. I was a little frustrated because I thought his long-term goal was to be a teacher and a coach. *Had he quit on himself again*? No. I later understood that joining the air force was the smartest move he ever made because it kept him well clear of the drugs, alcohol, and crime that haunted him. That military discipline forced him to get his life squared away and forced him to look inside himself to deal with all of that pain in a constructive manner.

While in the service, he earned his BA in social work and returned to Southern California as a counselor in a juvenile facility. Funny, he is working with kids who are much like he was. He also helped me coach and work with some of the more troubled wrestlers. He is now a social worker and Sunday school teacher in Tacoma, Washington; married with a baby boy. Most importantly, Ronnie got his life right with the Lord again. He now at times counsels me spiritually and quotes Bible scriptures I once taught him. He is not making the same harmful decisions that he made ten years ago, but he has to live with the tough memory of those negative choices. Nevertheless, my memories of Ronnie will never fade.

Ronnie came a long way in his young life, and I am enormously proud of him. I love him like a son, forgive him for his misdeeds, and plan to maintain our relationship for many years to come.

Reflections on Ronnie

Forgiveness—that's what Ronnie taught me—only I learned it the hard way. It's difficult to forgive someone who has lied to you, defied you, and let you down. It really hurts when someone you care about causes you great pain. It was hard for me to forgive him and not hold a grudge, but then I remembered the Bible verse Matthew 18:21. "'Lord how many times shall I forgive my brother when he sins against me? Up to seven times?' Jesus answered, 'I tell you not seven times, but seventy-seven times'" (NIV). So I did just that.

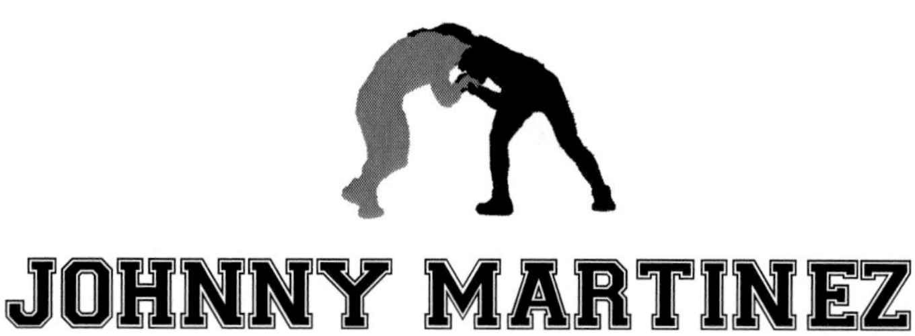

JOHNNY MARTINEZ

1990–1994

> One needs something to believe in, something for which one can have whole-hearted enthusiasm. One needs to feel that one's life has meaning, that one is needed in this world.
>
> —Hannah Senesh (Jewish diarist, poet, and playwright)

The first season at Santa Ana High School was a difficult one. The biggest problem was just putting a squad together and trying to win some matches. That was half the battle. The other half was dealing with the individual athletes, because most of them did not understand what it meant to be dedicated. They did not know what it would take to be their best. Still, I had some students on the team who had the talent to be great wrestlers—they just lacked the motivation. It was frustrating to see all that talent and potential without desire. It is safe to say that I wanted their success for them more than they did for themselves.

One student who had all of that ability without the fire was Johnny Martinez. He was enrolled in my sixth-period wrestling class, though I rarely saw him because he had a severe attendance problem. The first time I actually saw him, he stood five feet four inches, with a very lean build. He was quiet and reserved. Looking at Johnny, one would assume that his life was better than a lot of the athletes on the team. He was well groomed and seemed healthy, but sometimes kids can give off the impression that everything is better than it really is. However, some kids from the inner city of Santa Ana generally were not okay emotionally—and Johnny fit that description.

Only a few freshmen came out for the sport my first year as coach, so when Johnny with his junior high wrestling experience decided to come out, I saw some hope for the program. All aspirations for him quickly dwindled because he had such problems with attendance and responsibility. He was rarely in school, there was little time to form any relationship with him, and he made no time to establish a relationship with the team. No one really had any answers as to where he was or why he was not attending school regularly. He showed up a couple of times a month, but I could never get any answers out of him because he was a quiet person by nature.

I grew more frustrated with his attendance issues and lack of responsiveness. I confess that the frustration led me to treat him with less grace and respect. Since I could not reach him or get any identifiable information out of him, I regrettably resorted to picking on him. When he did finally show up to school, I would give it to him hard. "If you don't straighten out your life and get back into school, you'll end up a bum, and I am sure your mom will be real proud of you then!"

I hoped that by berating him he would get back into school, but that technique failed. At that time, Santa Ana High had very little in terms of an attendance policy. In fact, attendance was horrific, with about one-third of all students showing up late—if at all. Several students were notorious for leaving school and heading to Mexico to visit family. Those absences would last for months, so Johnny's problems never really raised a flag. He was just one of many such lost kids. With all the fires I had to put out on the team, I simply could not find the time to deduce why Johnny missed so much school. I was still approaching the Santa Ana kids with the same philosophy under which I wrestled—that, if a kid was serious about wrestling, he would be in school doing what he needed to do.

In time, I realized most of them needed some source of accountability and an authority figure that cared. Unfortunately, many of their adult role models, including parents, brothers, and sisters, gave up on them. It became a matter of showing that someone cared. I did not communicate that to Johnny as soon as I should have in our relationship. I let him fall by the wayside and did not focus on him when he was not in school. Later on, I figured out how to reach him and focused on keeping him in school while motivating him to become a better student.

As I spent more time with him, I finally learned his history. An only child, he was born in El Salvador and lived there until age six. His parents moved to the U.S. to escape the war that rocked the country in the 1980s. They hoped to save enough money and gain residency to bring him to the U.S.

Johnny lived with an aunt in El Salvador for the two years his parents were away. The details of his young life are a bit fuzzy. However, he remembers the country being humid and sticky with lush rainforests. He also remembers dusty dirt roads and small homes with no indoor plumbing. He was bathed by standing in an outdoor tub while his mother poured buckets of cold water over him. There was no refrigerator, so they had to purchase fresh food daily.

He recalls a time when he almost severely injured his hand when a firework he held exploded. His aunt ran cold water over his throbbing, red hand and coated it with soothing aloe vera. The explosion of the firework was so close to his ear that it left him temporarily deaf with a ringing in his ears. He was very frightened because he could not hear what others were saying.

In 1981, his mother returned for him. She hired a "coyote," a highly paid smuggler of illegal aliens, to get her, Johnny, his mother, an uncle, and a family friend back into the U.S. They made the long and dangerous journey from El Salvador, through Guatemala and Mexico, into the United States. Johnny does not remember much of the trek, leading him to believe he must have been asleep and carried most of the way. One event that does stick out in his mind, however, is a night they all crouched under some dried bushes as border patrol and police helicopter circled overhead. He remembers bright spotlights, the wind, and dirt blowing all around them. They were subsequently arrested by border patrol authorities.

Fortunately, his mother had enough money to cover bail. Also at that time, President Reagan allowed Salvadoran refugees to enter the U.S. due to the ongoing civil war. As a result, they were soon released from INS detention and reunited with his father. After he told his story, I asked why his father sent his mother, his own wife, on such a long and dangerous mission, rather than handle it himself. It seemed like a husband's responsibility to protect his wife while escorting their son across international borders patrolled by armed guards. Johnny remained silent about his father's decision.

After years of waiting, Johnny gained full citizenship. Unfortunately, during that time, he watched his parents drift apart and eventually divorce when it became clear that his father was secretly visiting a girlfriend in El Salvador at every opportunity. *After the divorce, Johnny lived with his mother, bouncing from one run-down apartment to another. She remarried, and he found himself alienated from her affection, as he was no longer the most important person in her life. I believe many of his problems began at that point.* What difference did school or wrestling make when he was losing his mother?

Throughout the first three years of high school, he was rarely in school. However, he did enjoy wrestling and often came to practice, though irregularly. Sadly, his attendance led to grades that were so poor they interfered with his wrestling eligibility. My frustration grew with his self-defeating behavior. As a last ditch effort, I had him tested for special education, hoping that might help to identify his problems and perhaps improve his school performance. I do not think he appreciated the effort, since it embarrassed him and wounded his adolescent pride.

Nevertheless, we attended a meeting with the student review board, consisting of the principal, the school nurse, an outreach consultant counselor, an academic counselor, and one of Johnny's teachers. We grilled him as to why he did not attend school. His mother also sat in with the group, and while she seemed willing to help, she appeared helpless to turn Johnny around academically. After the meeting, I feared that we did not get anywhere with him. Indeed, he went right back into his lazy ways. His diagnostic test scores proved too high for special education, so he was never a candidate for the program. He was a bright kid, but he refused to apply himself. A lack of self-esteem convinced him that he simply could not function.

Johnny's desperation to gain his mother's full attention grew even worse when he learned that she was pregnant with his stepfather's child. The thought of another child in the family—a baby that would certainly demand all of his mother's attention—drove him to give up on school almost entirely.

When the baby arrived, the family moved to a nicer apartment complex in Costa Mesa. Perhaps not all was as bleak as he feared between Johnny and his mother. He seemed to show renewed interest in Santa Ana High and the wrestling team. In fact, he began to train on a regular basis, significantly improving his wrestling.

I made a deal with him to pick him up and drive him to school every day if he would get up and make the effort to get to school and earn better grades. Johnny's new effort yielded a C average, a real shock since Fs ruled his report cards for much of his academic life. Still, there were those days when he would not wake up for school, and I would go wake him up by irritably pounding on the door waiting for him to open it. His parents left early for work before he got up, so I got no help from them. One morning, as I peeked through the window, I caught a glimpse of him scampering down the hall, hiding, instead of answering the door. I can only imagine what the neighbors thought of me: a stranger pounding on the door and peering through the windows. It was embarrassing at times, but I needed to get him in school.

He was, however, having a good senior season, emerging as one of the top wrestlers on the team. Assistant Coach Vince Silva, an All-American at Oklahoma State, took an interest in him and believed he could become a legitimate Division I NCAA wrestler. Silva hoped to earn Johnny a scholarship to Arizona State in Phoenix because he knew the head wrestling coach there. Sadly, Johnny showed no interest in attending college, and he never got the grades necessary for college admission. He had the mental toughness in the wrestling room, but it did not carry over into the classroom.

He finished his senior season as a league champion and received second place at the CIF Southern Section Championships. (CIF is an acronym for the California Interscholastic Federation, which is a nonprofit corporation organized to administer athletics in secondary schools within its membership and geographical boundaries.) He was third in the Masters Meet, the qualifying tournament for the California State Championships, which earned him a shot at wrestling in the State Championships. That was his goal during his senior year. Unfortunately, once he met that goal, he quit. It never failed to amaze me how someone could work an entire season to get into an event and then totally collapse once he arrived. I suppose I had no right to expect more from him. I got more out of him than I ever hoped I could and to think he could have placed in state was a dream I had that he did not share.

After wrestling season, Johnny's motivation to continue attending Santa Ana High immediately died. He never woke up again for his ride to school, and when he gave up, so did I, because I could not force him to go to school, though I had hoped his wrestling commitment might carry over until graduation.

I worried what would become of him. In fact, I heard that he was out wandering the streets of Santa Ana late one evening and was mugged. Two thugs accosted him. One had a gun pointed to his chest, the other with a knife in his back. Johnny gave them the few dollars he had in his pocket and the jean jacket he was wearing. Would this mugging ever have happened if Johnny had stayed in school and been focused on his academics? He was a smart but lost kid with unlimited potential. How much contact would I still have with him? Would I ever hear from him again? Strangely enough, not only did Johnny stick around, but also we occasionally did things together, and our relationship remains intact today. While I was discouraged that he never finished school or pursued collegiate wrestling, I never held a grudge or any ill will toward him.

His life became a string of dead-end jobs, ranging from assembly lines to customer service. Fortunately, the string of failures convinced him that he was not getting anywhere but older. Somewhere along the line, he discovered an interest in computers, and finally embraced something that seemed to motivate him. He was willing to work to gain computer skills in technical school. I had not seen him so excited since he left the wrestling mat. It was good to see him energized about something, especially such a potentially lucrative career. In no time, he was racking up technical certifications. In less than two years, he studied on his own and passed a series of tests that had him in line for successful, high-tech employment.

This time, Johnny's timing could not have been better. I knew the owner of a large software company who needed someone to troubleshoot the several hundred computers it purchased for its new network. I introduced Johnny to the owner and he volunteered for several hours of work to gain experience and a shot at a full-time job in the corporate world. Once again, I was picking him up every day—now it was for work and dropping him off on my way to school. He was not a struggling student but a valued employee of a large company. He got out of bed this time.

Many people ask why I did not give up on him, but Johnny was not the kind of young man I *wanted* to give up on, especially when he finally found his niche in life. I got more from him than he ever got from me. Most of all, I enjoy the pride of seeing him turn it all around.

He reentered the wrestling world, helping some of my wrestlers from time to time and assisting me with tournaments. He went from being a kid I could not get out of bed a few years earlier to a man who found his purpose in life.

Reflections on Johnny

Johnny helped me realize that every man needs a purpose in his life. Johnny was the one wrestler who frustrated me the most. His talent surpassed that of all others I'd coached, yet his desire to use it did not exist. I did everything in my power to get the most out of him. It wasn't until I saw Johnny's interest in computers that I figured he just needed a purpose to get his life moving. Working with computers defined who he was and gave his life direction. I now understand that each wrestler I coach needs a purpose in life to be fulfilled. Sometimes wrestling is not that purpose; however, the sport may just be the means to find it.

ROGER SANTIAGO-GLABB'S SON

1990–1994

> Feeling gratitude and not expressing it is like wrapping a present and not giving it.
>
> —William Arthur Ward, writer of inspirational maxims

I first heard of Roger when his PE teacher told me he had a tough, naturally athletic specimen in his class. He was rippled with muscles from head to toe, and with his dark skin tone, every muscle stood out. His body was more like a body builder's. At only five feet three inches, he was solid and clearly intimidating to anyone close to the same size.

After the conversation with the PE teacher, I never thought once about Roger, until one day I entered the wrestling room and saw him warming up for tryouts. He was very quiet, but his presence spoke for him. *Finally*, I thought. I had an athlete who gave me hope that I could shape his body and mind into that of a real wrestler.

Part of me was excited about having a real wrestler on the team, someone who could really compete…And then I saw his long black hair. Back in the early 1990s, there were clear rules on hair length—it had to be collar length and above the ears. Roger was nowhere near these standards.

I figured that once he found out that his long mane would need cutting he would quit the team. Fortunately, he came in a few days later with a new, clean-cut style. He obviously wanted to wrestle more than I thought.

He was shy and extremely quiet—so much so that one of his teachers feared he did not speak English. He was actually fluent in both English and Spanish. For some reason, I was drawn to Roger, hoping to mentor and teach him toward becoming a great wrestler and a good man. I took him under my wing, to the point that the other wrestlers noticed and referred to him as Glabb's son.

He had no knowledge of his father and would not recognize him if he stood in the same room with him. Roger lived about a block from the high school in what was once a bedroom in a much larger home—a beautiful old home in a community that declined around it. It was remodeled into a small apartment complex.

Roger's mother, sister, brother, and his brother's wife all lived with him in the second-story apartment. It was first come, first served for sleeping arrangements, and Roger often found himself sleeping in the bathroom. It was depressing to see his tough living conditions and how cramped it must have been for him, but it was home to him, and he never complained.

Since he was without a father and had brothers in and out of trouble with the law, I took it upon myself to spend time with Roger. We often went to movies together and played video games. One afternoon, Roger and I headed to 7-Eleven. We were involved in a game of video baseball when I heard the cashier dump out a bunch of change. As long as the clerk had change out, I decided I would get a few more quarters so we could continue a while longer. I turned to the counter and saw a man in black-rimmed glasses pointing a gun at the cashier.

Our eyes locked, and he said, "Do not make a move, or I'll shoot."

I will never forget the look on his face. He was clearly psychotic or high. Here I was, a corn-fed white man from Washington State, and I had never seen a robbery in progress before, let alone faced the end of a gun barrel. I was terrified and turned away, pretending to go back to the game. I never experienced fear like that, and I definitely felt my life was in immediate danger.

I told Roger the store was being robbed and warned him not to do anything. He was consumed in the game as I prayed silently for protection. It surprised him a little.

Protecting Roger was also foremost on my mind. The counter was over my right shoulder. I glanced over to see the robber leave and jump into his car. I rushed outside to get a license plate number, but it was too late. There was no Sylvester Stallone or Steven Segal moment. When you are staring at a gun and afraid for your life, all you can really think about is staying alive. During the crisis, Roger did not seem particularly disturbed. Some of that was his experience on the streets, and the rest of it was his innate toughness.

On the mat, it did not take long for him to excel as a wrestler. By the end of his sophomore year, he was one of the top wrestlers in the area, and we grew closer as coach and team member. Slowly, his wall of silence wore away, and he felt comfortable enough to open up about his past, sharing the trials of growing up in a single-parent home in Santa Ana. I learned that one of his live-in brothers was a gang member. I felt pride that Roger himself never fell into that trap. He used wrestling as a way to keep focused on school and to stay off the streets.

The finest memory of coaching Roger was during his sophomore year when the team was wrestling a dual meet against La Habra High School. In a dual meet, there are two teams wrestling each other with fourteen wrestlers, one wrestler representing each weight class.

Roger finished winning his match and then sat beside me on the team bench. I was doing my coaching thing, yelling and screaming to the other athletes out on the mat.

In the middle of it all, Roger looked at me and said, "Coach, I love you." I was completely taken aback. There I was, a young coach trying to build a program, encountering many strange things in a short time, but no education class or coaching experience ever prepared me for hearing something like this from one of my wrestlers.

I felt awkward. I had a fifteen-year-old kid who clearly looked up to me as a father figure. He put himself out on a limb and took a risk, allowing himself to be vulnerable enough to say the three hardest words—the three words a young man his age would otherwise probably never say to an adult male.

My mind raced to find the right answer. It seemed like several minutes passed before I came up with one, but it was really only a few seconds. Roger needed to hear those words back. If I blew it or changed the subject, he would be hurt and maybe withdraw. Perhaps he would never take a risk like that again with anyone.

"Hey, I love you too."

"Coach, I was just kidding!" he exclaimed

That threw me a little, but it is what one might expect from a young man at that moment. I chuckled and returned to coaching. He was not joking. He meant it but needed to save face after opening up so much. I believe it was just his way of saying thank you. He was expressing his gratitude for me being more than a coach to him.

Roger and I remained close throughout his high school career.

He excelled as a wrestler, making a name for himself as an athlete in Southern California. We were optimistic for him as his junior year arrived. His goal was to become a state qualifier—a great achievement in California, especially for a student who just started the sport less than three years earlier.

California has more than seven hundred high schools with wrestling programs, so being a state qualifier means as much to any wrestler as *placing* in other state championships. Most states have high schools split up into five or six divisions of wrestling to water down the competition. The mammoth state of California has only *one* division.

Roger's goal of making state that junior year fell a little short. It helps to understand the physical commitment and time dedication needed to become a top-level wrestler. Roger paid his dues, and he was owed that trip to state, but he did not quite make it. He was extremely discouraged, and I understood his disappointment, never having qualified for state myself while wrestling in Washington.

Unfortunately, he got so down on himself that it put a chip on his shoulder and he threatened to quit wrestling and try out for basketball. It was an empty threat considering his five-foot-three-inch height, but he played many pickup games, so he thought it was possible. Eventually reality set in, and he realized he had too much invested in wrestling. He had the potential to be one of the greatest wrestlers in Santa Ana High School's history.

True to form, his senior year proved his best yet. By postseason, he won his third-consecutive league championship and became our school's first Division I CIF champion, defeating wrestlers from more than seventy other schools. At the Masters Meet, the competition that qualifies wrestlers for state, Roger finished a solid fourth and finally won his berth to the state championships.

The following weekend, we headed to Stockton, California, for the State Championships at the University of the Pacific, in an arena holding approximately seven thousand people, which can prove quite intimidating for a young man who never saw an arena that size, let alone *competed* in one.

Along with Roger came Miguel and Ronald, two other seniors who qualified in their respective weight classes. The first thing every coach does when arriving at state is register, check the wrestlers' individual weights, and begin working out. That is exactly what we did.

While Roger was in high school, the weight classes for competition were 103, 112, 119, 125, 130, 135, 140, 145, 152, 160, 171, 189, and 275. By the late 1990s, the National Federation of State High School Associations saw a need to add the 215-pound weight class to its classifications to give more athletes the opportunity to compete.

Roger was a natural 103-pound wrestler for his first three years of competition. However, as a senior growing into young adulthood, he usually needed to get down to wrestling weight from 115 pounds. That is a significant weight cut for anyone his size with a body-fat percentage of maybe 5 percent.

As he stepped on the scale, I gasped. He was eight pounds over the limit, with less than eighteen hours to official weigh-ins. If he did not make weight, he would lose his opportunity. I was worried, but I did not see that same fear in his face. He knew he would make weight, so I left him alone to cut the weight his own way.

Part of what makes wrestling perhaps the most grueling of high school sports is weight cutting. Making the required weight for the sport can take the fun out of it. Worrying about weight during the season is more burdensome than failing grades, family problems, or broken relationships. As a wrestler in high school and college, I recall the worrying and paranoia that would drive me to sleepless, stomach-churning nights just waiting for the weigh-in. After that key moment, I would pig out, even though the worrying would continue with the next tournament or match, a burden that stuck throughout the season and sometimes into the off-season.

Some wrestlers run the risk of developing eating disorders after years of weight cutting. Before you know it, it possesses you. I did not envy Roger's quest to lose eight pounds. I expected it would be especially hard for someone of his height and lean structure.

Losing that amount of weight can cause an athlete to become weak and to wrestle poorly in his first match of a tournament. Knowing Roger would step onto the mat just after weigh-ins, I feared he would prove too fatigued and drained to wrestle well during the first round of competition.

He made the weight at 103 pounds first thing the next morning. When I was cutting weight in high school, it took me a week to lose eight pounds. He made it look easy.

"Are you too weak to wrestle?" I asked.

"I am ready," he grinned

His first match pitted him against one of the top-rated wrestlers in his weight class. I thought he had no chance of beating him after his weight struggles. I tried to instill the confidence he would need to beat a competent opponent, but deep down, I had a feeling that it would not happen. Too many factors ran against Roger.

What would I say if he lost? I had to prepare myself for that possibility although all the worry disappeared because, yet again, he surprised me. He wrestled one of his best matches of the year and won. He beat his second opponent more easily than the first. Then, the third match pitted him against a familiar face, another wrestler from our neck of the woods.

Though they had never wrestled each other, I knew the athlete was a formidable opponent and would not make it easy on Roger. He soon found himself in a killer of a match. As he was going into the final twenty seconds of the third and final round, the match was tied, three to three. Roger wanted to work for a fall or perhaps take the match into a two-minute, sudden death overtime. That was the strategy. But Roger was penalized a point, with less than twenty seconds remaining in the match, for failing to start in the proper position, a simple mental error. He trailed four to three, and it seemed as if it were over.

Roger could only let his opponent up for a one-point escape and try for a two-point takedown to tie the match. It is amazing how many thoughts I had racing through my mind in twenty seconds. *Will he do it? Did I make the right coaching decisions? Should he have stayed on top of him and tried to turn him although his opponent was a cagey veteran? How could Roger have made such a simple mistake?*

That stream of consciousness disappeared in a flash with fewer than ten seconds to go as Roger dug deep and somehow found the strength to take his opponent down onto his back for a five-point score and victory.

Although it was just the quarterfinals, the emotion Roger showed on the edge of that wrestling mat said it all. With that win, it guaranteed him a top six finish at state. He was now the *first* Santa Ana High School state place-winner.

The semi-finals offered his toughest challenge of the season in the form of the number-one ranked wrestler in California. His opponent had beaten him badly the year before, and he wore an air of arrogance against anyone he wrestled. He could be viciously and unnecessarily rough. Still, when Roger stepped onto the mat, he showed a confidence I admit I did not share.

I waited for his opponent to unleash that explosiveness, but Roger held his own, keeping the match close. Unfortunately, we faced one of the most regrettable moments of my coaching career just seconds later.

His opponent clearly became frustrated, maybe even frightened, that Roger might interfere with his quest for a state championship. He knew he was the undisputed favorite, and the possibility of failure obviously did not sit well with him.

Off a nice double leg takedown on Roger, he lifted Roger off the mat and slammed him down angrily, square on the shoulder. Roger had struggled with injuries to that shoulder throughout the season. Perhaps his opponent knew that because the referee considered this an illegal move and penalized him a point.

When someone in a wrestling match is injured with an illegal move, the injured wrestler receives two minutes to recover. During that time, the tournament doctor or trainer diagnoses the injury and determines whether that wrestler can continue. If he cannot, the injured wrestler will be awarded the win via forfeit because his opponent caused injury by use of an illegal move.

When Roger was slammed, he had bounced back up and was ready to wrestle. However, I could see him holding his shoulder in agony. I wanted him to take the two minutes to examine his shoulder while I explained the situation. If he was too hurt to continue, he won the match. If he tried to compete and could not due to pain, he would lose the contest.

Perhaps this was too heavy a burden, too great a decision, for a high school senior to make. We both knew the state championship match loomed just ahead. I was blind for those two minutes and really wanted that finals match, but Roger was a competitor and wanted to wrestle. I believe I subliminally persuaded him to make the decision to take the easy win against his wishes.

With tears of confusion in his eyes, he took the match on a forfeit for the illegal move, saying he was too hurt to continue. I know he would have gotten back out there if I had not influenced him to make that decision, I told myself at the time it was the right thing to do and I was looking out for the safety of my wrestler.

Imagine, seven thousand seats full of spectators anticipating what would happen in a key semifinal match. They believed Roger would continue and not try to steal his opponent's desire for a state championship. He did not.

Do I wish Roger never would have got hurt? Yes.

Do I feel bad for the other wrestler who lost? Yes.

Do I want to relive that moment over again and do things different? Yes.

But sometimes a coach's desire to win supersedes his values and morals ... a desire I know every coach feels at least once during his coaching career. Sometimes, in that moment, he loses sight of the right thing to do.

When the referee raised Roger's hand, the elation of winning was replaced by dread as all I heard were boos cascading from the stands. No doubt the fans thought I told Roger to take the win. The crowd was ruthless, and Roger's opponent threw a fit. His coaches stood by, shocked to realize their certain state championship was gone. The best he could do was third place. As I walked off the arena floor, I heard:

"That's bull*&@#!"

"I can't believe you did that!"

"You are a joke!"

"You should be ashamed!"

Their eyes stayed on Roger and me as we walked out of the arena. I felt like the pariah of wrestling coaches, as my peers looked ashamed of me. We headed to the tournament doctor. He examined Roger's arm and shoulder with aggressive tugs, obviously angry and disappointed with the outcome of the match.

"He could have wrestled," the doctor said.

With that, the doctor walked out of the room. I felt he clearly lacked the compassion he could have had for his patient. This doctor had an agenda that did not include the health of the athletes in the tournament.

I was sick to my stomach for the rest of the day, afraid to show my face among the fans and coaches. Roger and I sneaked back to the hotel and I lay in bed churning over what happened. Since we did not need to get back to the arena for six hours, I had plenty of time to beat myself up for that decision.

As soon as we stepped back inside the arena, the fans greeted Roger with sneers and catcalls. During pre-match warm-ups for the finals, no one would drill or warm-up with him, leaving him to loosen up alone. I felt awful for him, responsible for his sudden exile.

The 103-pound finals were typically the first championship match of the night and got the crowd going in a lively mood. Usually it is an electric, party atmosphere honoring the sport. Not that night. The crowd was ugly and belligerent as the 103-pound star they came to see was sitting in the stands.

As Roger took the mat, rubber super balls flooded the court from the seats. It was sad and tragic, because ever since he was a freshman, I had envisioned him in the finals of a state championship. That moment came but felt nothing like what I imagined. With so much pressure and bitterness thrown his way, he did not wrestle his best and lost nine to three in front of seven thousand people eager to see him fall.

For Roger, his dream ended in heartache, pain, and embarrassment. I never discussed that day with him. Perhaps sometime I will get the opportunity to ask him what he felt like out there at the state championship match. Somehow I doubt we will ever cross that topic again.

Late into his senior year, a local high school wrestling coach, John Azevedo, asked if I had a senior wrestler on the team who could use a good job at a software company. Roger was the first to come to mind with his discipline and dedication. If he took his athletic commitment into the working world, he would prove an outstanding employee.

By that summer, after graduating high school, Roger held a full-time job with the aforementioned software company. Word got back to me on what a great worker he was, and he slowly worked his way up in the company. He started a family and settled down in the area.

I think I found myself envying Roger when I found him driving a Mercedes and making more than me in a year! However, that only lasted seconds because I knew I played a part in helping him get to where he was. Who knows where he would be without the sport of wrestling in his life. Perhaps he would be out on the street with his brother, or maybe he would be dead because of some senseless gang attack.

Changing lives like Roger's is one of the reasons I continue to coach. Although coaching will never make me materially rich, I remind myself that lives I touch will make me rich in spirit.

Reflections on Roger

It was Roger who first said, "I love you, Coach." Now, after several years of coaching at Santa Ana High School, I hear those words almost daily. It's usually at the end of the day or at the close of practice when I hear some of my wrestlers say, "Love you, Glabb" as they scurry out of the wrestling room. It is at that moment I am reminded how important and valued I am ... something any teacher or coach would want to feel. Roger made me feel worthy that day he said those three words, and he taught me that it is okay to express how you feel and show gratitude to someone who has touched your life.

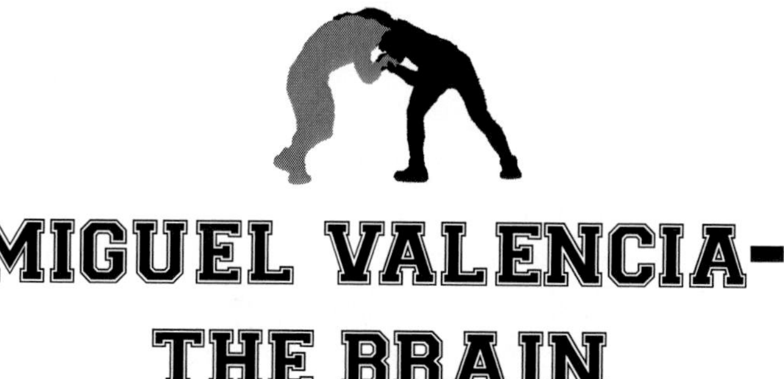

MIGUEL VALENCIA-THE BRAIN

1990–1994

It's choice—not chance—that determines your destiny.
—Jean Nidetch,
founder of the Weight Watchers organization

Miguel was another wrestler who made a big impact on my life. Of all the wrestlers I coached in the past, he was one of my favorites. His sarcastic nickname was the Brain, short for brain surgeon because he always made poor decisions and wrong choices. I mean how bright can a person be when they decide to put battery acid on a skin infection (ringworm?) You could imagine what kind of hole the acid left in his arm after practicing medicine on himself. He was not the sharpest tool in the shed, but he was really loveable and congenial to his teammates and me.

Miguel was five feet four inches and was a light-skinned, handsome Hispanic teen. In fact, he could almost pass for a Caucasian until he spoke. His English was extremely poor and difficult to understand when he conversed. I had no idea how long he had been in the U.S. when I met him. I knew his family was living here but were not citizens. He had seventeen brothers and sisters. With a family that size, he spent most of his time vying for attention from his parents. He met with little success. It confirmed what I worried about while coaching him: he was another kid without a real home.

Miguel tried out for the wrestling team because he loved Lucha Libre—the masked, high-flying Mexican version of professional wrestling. In fact, at the beginning of his high school career, he actually was a much better Lucha Libre–style wrestler than he was a collegiate, competitive wrestler.

I cannot pinpoint the first time I met him, but I recall him staying after practice, standing around the wrestling room with his shirt off flexing in the mirrors lining the far wall. He would pose as if he was in a Mr. Universe pageant. I think he kept doing it because we all thought it was funny and it gave him the sort of attention he craved.

The first conversation I remember with him was during his freshman year. He wanted to wrestle Martin, another athlete on the team. Martin was more experienced than him, and I foresaw trouble.

One of the beauties of coaching wrestling is the "wrestle-off," a match that determines who the varsity wrestler will be. Coaches do not select the members or assign positions as they do in other sports such as football, basketball, and baseball. Basically, a member of the team challenges the current varsity competitor for his spot. This is how the varsity wrestler in each weight class is determined—through a wrestle-off. Whoever wins the best two out of three matches assumes the varsity position for that weight class. In this case, Miguel wanted to challenge Martin at 119 pounds for an upcoming tournament.

"No problem," I said. After all, it is a coach's responsibility to encourage that sort of competitiveness, even though I knew Martin had a lot more wrestling experience.

They hit the mat, and the match lasted all of thirty seconds, with Martin easily pinning his younger opponent. Minutes after the match, I heard Miguel say in strained English, "Hey, Coach, I will let Martin wrestle for me this weekend at 119 pounds."

"I hope so, Miguel, seeing as he just kicked your butt."

I was amused by the whole thing and maybe even encouraged by his guts. He was a knucklehead, but he had an innocence about him that made it impossible not to enjoy his company. He was easily one of the most entertaining wrestlers I have ever coached. I recalled sitting at the corner of the mat during a tournament, yelling and screaming as coaches do. Miguel was wrestling and clearly winning his match. It was a rare sight to see. I shouted for him to try an inside cradle, a wrestling move to score a pin.

"Shhh!" he put his finger to his lips. That was beyond odd. I shouted the order again.

"Shhh!" he put his finger to his lips again.

"What are you doing? Why are you telling me to 'shhh'?" I pulled him aside after he won the match and asked. "You do not tell me to be quiet in the middle of a match!"

"But, Coach, you tell him my move. Do not tell him my move! It is a secret, Coach. Do not tell him my move."

A part of me was upset about being told what to do by one of my students, but I had to laugh. He was the only wrestler, and remains the only one, who told me to shut up during a match because I might give some secret strategy away.

Miguel struggled throughout his freshman year and was pounded on quite a bit. I shifted him between weight classes all season long, but to no avail. The beatings kept coming. His prospects dramatically turned around during his sophomore year as he significantly improved and became a very competitive athlete. It was as if some magical metamorphosis came over him during the summer, and he returned to the team a very skilled wrestler.

The change became obvious at the first tournament of the

year—a meet in which Miguel wrestled junior varsity during the previous year. Prior to then, I doubt he scored a point throughout the tournament. That year he wrestled nine matches in only two days and won almost all of them as a varsity wrestler. He finally lost to an outstanding challenger from Channel Islands in his last match of the tournament. We could not believe his progression, taking second place in a tournament of that size. Alas, second place for Miguel wasn't good enough. So to prove he was deserving of number one and the toughest kid at his weight class, he took his second place medal and pinned it to his bare chest. Ouch! With his shirt off and drops of blood dribbling down his torso, Miguel paraded around the gym, showing off his new hardware. I was just about ready to scold him for his foolish actions, and then I remembered whom I was dealing with: the Brain. It was another one of those Miguel moments that we all just had to laugh off.

After the tournament, the local newspaper that did a weekly ranking of each weight class in the county, ranked him fourth at his weight of 125 pounds. Unfortunately, the name read Mike instead of Miguel because he was a newcomer—the paper probably did not know his real name. When he read that, he did not understand that it was his first name mentioned in the paper until we explained it to him and what it meant.

Nevertheless, kids are kids, and the ranking went right to his head. In a match against Westminster, a rival team in our league that beat us the previous year fifty-three to eight, we gathered at weigh-ins before the dual meet. Miguel came waltzing in with sunglasses on and a towel draped around his neck. He did a little cocky boxing shuffle to show off in front of the other wrestlers. I do not think anyone else on the opposing team knew he was ranked. Still, he wanted to show everyone that he was "the man." Unfortunately, he embarrassed himself in the process.

I walked over to him, snatched the sunglasses off his face, and threw the towel aside. I berated him with the hard fact that you should never get that cocky. More importantly, you should never show up your teammates like that. After that little discussion, he went on the mat and wrestled the sloppiest, ugliest match I had ever seen from him. He got himself outright pinned later in the round.

Disappointment shrouded his face as he sensed the disillusionment from the entire team. We lost the match by a single point. Being a young coach, I blamed the loss on him. It was unfair, but I was still smarting from his sudden arrogance over his ranking. I needed to remember that I was working with fourteen-, fifteen- and sixteen-year-old kids. No one knew what they were thinking at one particular moment in time. Whether it was right or wrong, I put all my hopes, dreams, and desires onto the shoulders of these young athletes as they walk onto the mat. I prayed they would have the same goals, thoughts, and desire to win as I did. Sometimes they didn't.

That day, both Miguel and I learned a tremendous lesson, and we grew closer as player and coach as time passed. I do not think I became like a father to him, per se, but perhaps I played the role of an older brother. I took him in and fed him when he did not have any money, which, unfortunately, was almost all the time. I gave him some of my T-shirts and other clothes to wear to school. I grew very fond of him and knew that he was one of the boys in the program that really needed someone to support him.

At the same time, he was a student I could rely on at any time. He was not afraid of being coached. He would ask advice on anything and was always the first to offer if there was anything that needed to be done. Though still a student wrestler, he almost took on the role of an assistant coach.

One evening, I was home with some friends playing a board game, and around midnight, I got a call from the Santa Ana Police Department asking if I knew Miguel. He had a telephone number in his wallet that directed the authorities to call me if he met with any trouble. He was involved in a fight with one of his brothers, and his parents wanted to press charges. The police would consider doing so unless I agreed to take him in for the night because he obviously could not stay at home.

Of course I agreed though I was amazed that his own parents were willing to press charges against him, clearly showing favoritism for one son over another. Miguel later explained that his brother and the rest of his huge family (seventeen brothers and sisters) were up that night talking, yelling, and screaming. Imagine the noise a family that size can make even when they are *not* fighting. He got frustrated from lack of sleep. His frustration broke out into a full-blown argument with his brother that boiled over into a fight. Since his parents had no clue how to resolve the matter, they simply decided to make one of their sons go away for the night by calling the police.

A few days later, I took him home, and with the help of another wrestler who translated for me, I tried to communicate to his parents that Miguel was a young man who made mistakes but who also needed a pat on the back occasionally, like any other youth. He needed to feel welcomed and liked in his home. I explained what I did as a coach to aid him in that department and how it seemed to be successful in stopping him from "losing his cool." His parents appeared to understand and agreed to try reaching out more, promising to make an effort to pay him more attention and offer parental love.

Upon reflection, I believe Miguel faced more pain and adversity than any other wrestler on the team throughout my coaching career. His poor environment and some of his foolish, youthful decisions were huge obstacles to be surpassed. I sensed he needed more than just wrestling to help overcome this life of adversity. I invited him, along with some of the other wrestlers, to church, which he enthusiastically accepted.

Maybe he saw going to church as a way to get out of the house, but he seemed to enjoy it. He soon began to attend the weekly FCA (Fellowship of Christian Athletes) meetings we held after school and participated without hesitation in the skits and group studies we carried out at the meetings. Miguel even attended the FCA summer wrestling camp. There, he accepted Christ as his personal Savior and made a commitment to live a better lifestyle. However, when Miguel came back home and hit the streets, living the right life and making the right decisions became a difficult challenge.

Unfortunately, like Ronnie (Enano), Miguel was one of the wrestlers who spent time with the local transvestites in return for money, food, and shelter. While Ronnie did it more for entertainment and as a joke, Miguel turned to it for attention and recognition. Affirmation from transvestites was more than he was getting at home, even after I invited more concern and involvement from his parents.

Living in a gang-infested neighborhood did not help him. Jogging near his apartment in an attempt to cut weight for an upcoming meet one day, he ran into a group of gangbangers who jumped him and beat him up. They broke a couple of his ribs and left him cut up and bruised. His reaction was amazing. It was just another day in the neighborhood. He came to school looking as if he had been through a war zone and did not react with any significant trauma or shock; neither did anyone else on the team. Miguel could not wrestle the next day in our league match.

Nevertheless, as he improved as a wrestler, he became more of an asset to the team. I realized he might not be around for his senior year. Although I met him during what I believed was his freshman year, he had attended Santa Ana High School a year before but had to quit school to help his father, who fell out of a tree while working and was on disability.

Consequently, at the end of his junior season, Miguel was unable to compete his senior year because he had burned up his four years of high school eligibility. Though he did not compete that first year or even a semester, his junior season officially counted as his fourth year of school. The only exceptions to this rule are cases of personal hardships. I considered the incident with Miguel's father to be a clear case of that.

The only chance of success was compiling as much evidence as was available and being thorough in his appeal. I set about collecting all the paperwork on the injury his father sustained, contacting the doctor who treated him and the attorney who filed the disability case. Further, I got resulting work history for Miguel (not as easy as I anticipated,) including tax records from his place of work, and, finally, I included strong letters of recommendation from a school counselor and me explaining how deserving this young man was. I filed a case in the hope of getting his fourth year of eligibility back. Santa Ana High School's principal and athletic director warned me that I most likely would not get that year back from the CIF governing board that made those decisions. Very few hardships filed received approval.

The process took the entire summer before Miguel's senior season, but I kept the faith, as Miguel really wanted to wrestle his senior year. Strangely, I never felt lucky when it came to athletes struggling to stay in my program. It seemed that I lost them all too often from bad grades, poor attitudes, or a need to work to support their families. Maybe it was just a coach feeling frustrated, but it always seemed like I lost the very best athletes due to one cause or another.

Lady luck was on our side. The CIF governing board approved Miguel's appeal and cleared the way for a special senior season for him. Going the extra mile was worth it. As a senior, Miguel had come a long way, much further than I envisioned, having seen him when he first stepped onto the mat to challenge Martin four years earlier. He finished his career as a three-time league champion and a CIF southern-section divisional champion—a tournament that included, at the time, more than seventy other schools. He placed in the Masters Meet, which qualified him for the State Championships too. Not bad, considering he was one of the worst freshmen I ever saw when he walked through the door to exhibit his silly poses in front of the mirror.

As life would have it, when one obstacle is cleared, another one emerges. About three months away from graduation, Miguel was hanging out with one of his sister's male friends and another wrestler from the team. They were cruising one night and ended up running out of gas in Newport Beach. His sister's friend headed down to the beach to ask people for money, hoping to scrape up enough for the trip home. A short while later, Miguel saw the friend in a fight and went to help, only to find a man stabbed. His sister's buddy was carrying a knife and stabbed the victim when he refused to give up any money for gas.

They panicked and piled into the car, using whatever cash they robbed from the victim to buy their getaway gas. The police pulled them over because the car looked like one recently used in a nearby ATM robbery. Of course, they did not know that, and due to their nervousness, the police searched the car, found the knife, and took them to the station. Each one of them told a different a story, a fact that served to irritate the police, and they were thrown into jail.

I learned of this while reading the local crime reports in a Costa Mesa newspaper; it stated that three minors were involved in an attempted robbery and stabbing on the beach. When I read their descriptions, along with the make and model of the car, I realized two of them were from my wrestling program.

I was shocked, frustrated, and hurt that Miguel would be involved in something so foolish. Once again, I was writing letters on his behalf and appearing in court as a character witness whenever I could. Unfortunately, the case was repeatedly postponed, so I did not get a chance to help Miguel.

When I spoke to the public defender assigned to the case, it became clear that he was not enthusiastic about Miguel's chances in the matter. He dropped the ball, and Miguel was found guilty as part of a clumsy, rushed plea bargain.

Miguel spent the next few months in custody because he was not eighteen at the time of sentencing. He headed to Juvenile

Hall before being transferred to Orange County Jail and Wasco State Prison. Finally, the state transferred him, yet again, to the men's jail in Chino, California.

After seventeen months in the prison system, he was assigned to a jail in El Centro, California, which serves as a detention center for the INS, because he was not a U.S. citizen. There, he faced another trial that would decide his eligibility to remain in the United States. I headed toward the Mexico border.

I imagine few average folks have ever set foot in El Centro, but it is probably the closest place to hell on Earth. It is incredibly hot, barren, bleak, and desolate. It is a naturally desperate place, and the mix of frightened immigrants and hard-nosed criminals only makes that atmosphere worse. I was glad I was only going down there for a short time.

During the case, I wanted to speak on Miguel's behalf as a character witness, but the judge would have none of it. He asked Miguel if he committed the crime, and he denied any involvement. The judge reminded him of his plea bargain, essentially chastising him for copping his plea if he was innocent.

The judge finally ruled that he be deported to Mexico. I sat in the courtroom with his disheartened family and Ronnie. We protested as much as we could. His entire immediate family lived in Santa Ana. Where would Miguel go? Where would he live when he was a stranger in his own country?

A few weeks later, he called, explaining that he was in Tijuana and needed help again. Ronnie and I headed to Mexico. He was waiting at the border.

Miguel was staying in a shelter in Tijuana, washing windows to earn a few pesos, enough to avoid starving to death. It was sad to see our friend living this way; we felt powerless to help him. Unbeknownst to me, Miguel and Ronnie spoke to a few coyotes down there. In Mexico, coyotes are people who aid illegal immigrants in crossing the border. They found men willing to smuggle Miguel back across for about $700, but of course the boys didn't have that kind of money.

While Miguel and Ronnie were off on their clandestine mission, I went to the pharmacy to buy Miguel some toiletries he could use in his shelter. I had brought him some clothes, but he really needed some new shoes too. When the guys returned, we had lunch, and I handed Miguel some money to help him buy some food for the week. Then we made our way back to the border crossing, where we would say our good-byes. As we neared the crossing, Miguel, light-skinned and with improved English, shot ahead of us in line, approached the INS officer, and told him he was a U.S. citizen.

"Where's your ID?" the border patrol officer asked.

"I left it in the car," Miguel answered without missing a beat.

"Start praying, Coach," Ronnie leaned over and said to me. I froze, thinking, *What's he doing?*

"Well, then who are you with?"

Miguel pointed to us. The officer motioned us forward, checked our IDs, then waved all three of us through, across the border and back into the United States. I'm not sure if it was some kind of miracle or luck, but it was terrifying to me at the time. It occurred so quickly with little time for me to process or comprehend what just happened. Miguel essentially broke the law by lying to the officer. Who knows what my responsibility or liability would have been if it had turned out differently.

Several years later, Miguel and I discussed that bewildering day. He explained to me that he had no intention of trying to cross. In fact, he had told a friend of his from the shelter that he would be back before nightfall. Miguel's reaction at the border was unexpected, even for him. He was a desperate man who saw a chance and risked it. He ached to be home with family and friends again. Who could blame him?

He stayed with me for a couple of months and enrolled in a local junior college. Miguel wrestled a year at the college and placed sixth in the Junior College State Championships. He also spent a year as my assistant coach. Unfortunately, he never finished his coursework at the college because he met a girl and got married at age twenty-two. However, Miguel did get his GED (General Educational Development), which is the equivalent of a high school diploma, several years later.

Today, Miguel is living in Southern California. He has three children and works hard toward being a responsible husband and father. He is an honest young man, and despite his past problems, I am proud of him. I just sometimes wish he had made better choices earlier in his life. He keeps in touch and visits occasionally. It is satisfying to see him keeping it all together because I truly believe he was saved by the sport of wrestling.

Reflections on Miguel

Although Miguel didn't always make the best choices for his life, he was still one of my favorite wrestlers, not because he was a good wrestler or because he made me laugh. He was my favorite because he was a young man with a servant's heart. I often tell my wrestlers and students that there are only two kinds of people in the world. "There are the givers and there are the takers. Which one are you?" Most respond by saying they are a little of both. I respond back by telling them you can't waver in the middle; you are either one or the other. Without a doubt, Miguel was a giver. Miguel was the only wrestler who offered to help me mop the mats, clean the locker room, or carry my duffle bag at the end of a long day. One day I thought to myself, *Here is a kid who never received a Christmas or birthday gift from his family in the time I've known him, yet without hesitation, he'd spend his last dollar on a Gatorade for a teammate.* It always seems that the ones who have the least give the most. Miguel showed me the importance of serving my fellow man.

FERNANDO SERRATOS-RAT

1993–1997

> We all have big changes in our lives that are more or less a second chance.
>
> —Harrison Ford, American film actor

They called him Rat. I met Fernando, a.k.a. Rat, through his brother David, who joined wrestling during his sophomore year, my second season at Santa Ana High School. Darryl Killion, who was a special education teacher, had referred David. He thought he would benefit from the sport, since he was a little sidetracked. Apart from being talented, he had a problem with drinking and chasing girls, generally getting into trouble. Bad news seemed to follow him as fast as he could chase it. David was exposed to trouble at an early age.

David was often jumped on his way to and from school. When he made it home, it was to a small apartment, where he had to sleep in the hallway or on the living room floor because there were no beds left. There were too many family members wedged into the two-bedroom apartment.

David was tough to keep a handle on, as his behavior often shifted. There were times when he would show up to practice, and then he would disappear for two or three days. He was easily influenced and impacted by his friends' negativity. They often led him astray. Once, on a team trip to San Diego, we visited a bowling alley, and he disappeared, taking off with a friend. We found him at a park with a bunch of local girls. I later learned he had sex with one of them and contracted a venereal disease. David also got into trouble with the law.

On one occasion, when I picked David up for a visit to his parole officer, I met his brother, Fernando, and their mother, who accompanied us to his appointment. Fernando was in seventh grade, so he too was exposed to trouble at an early age.

Fernando was an all-round athlete, more so than David. He played baseball, football, and other sports. Fernando would occasionally come to wrestling practice with David and eventually took up the sport. He had a special ability and immediately picked up the moves. He continued to train with the team's wrestling club and officially came out for wrestling during the fall of his freshman year.

In that period, he followed his brother's path and hung out with the wrong crowd, spending time with a tagging crew (a group who spray paints graffiti on anything they could reach). This was a sad waste, as his knack for wrestling increased, he became skilled enough to wrestle on the varsity team as a freshman.

During Fernando's freshman year, I had an assistant coach Vince Silva. Having Vince in the wrestling room was a tremendous benefit to the program. He took the team to an entirely new level of wrestling. Coach Silva liked Fernando. It was he who nicknamed the freshman because he looked like a wet rat when soaked in sweat. Silva identified the special ability in him and invested his time and attention in the hope of developing his skills.

However, because he was hanging out with the wrong crowd, he eventually became ineligible to wrestle. It was sad and frustrating to see a student with so much ability throwing it all away with his tagging crew. He needed to learn that wrestling was where his attention needed to be. Fernando was someone to hang on to, a young man with the ability and character of a winner.

He also tended to be a genuine smart aleck, questioning everything I did as a coach. There are athletes that welcome guidance and input, but Fernando was a wrestler who felt driven to contradict everything I demanded of my athletes; he knew how to push my buttons. At one wrestling tournament, he angered me with comments that pushed me over the edge. We were nose to nose when I snapped at him, "Either you keep your smart mouth shut, or you can hit the road and find another team."

I regretted that moment and assumed that would be the last I saw of him, but the next day he was back in the wrestling room, training to get into shape for the next match. I must have slapped some sense into him. Sadly, that is often how it goes with troublemakers like him. They get into scrapes and smart off, but deep down they want someone to guide them, confront them, give them guidelines, and set boundaries.

His time commitment was still off though, and he came up with feeble excuses. I could write an entire second book on all of the lame excuses I have heard over the years from him as well as other wrestlers.

Of course, practice is hard, especially in wrestling. Athletes are cutting weight, working their butts off, putting in a lot of time and effort while fighting one opponent after another, but coming up with excuses to get out of practice does not make any wrestler better. This time, Fernando needed to "go home and vacuum" because his mother said so. I chuckled at that one.

At times, I believed he was a lost cause, much like his brother David. By the end of his freshman year, the question was whether or not he would continue wrestling after he had a rude awakening. Nearing the end of that year, the police arrested him for tagging a freeway sign. An officer walked Fernando to his front door and told his mother about the buildings, street signs, and freeway overpasses he had vandalized with graffiti.

For three years, Fernando spent his lunch money on spray paint, tucked the cans in his backpack, and went out to brazenly scribble his nickname "Ditto" across freeway signs in Santa Ana and surrounding cities during the brightest and busiest time of the day. Fernando's parents were very angry and disappointed, and they laid on him the biggest guilt trip of all, his family's story.

In 1977, Fernando's father left his wife, pregnant with Fernando, and two sons in León, Guanajuato, Mexico, and made the twelve hundred mile trek to El Monte, California. It was there when he held down two jobs, one as a stock person at an ol' Mom and Pop grocery store and the other as a landscaper shoveling dirt and planting trees. In two years Fernando's dad had saved over two thousand dollars, the price it cost for a coyote to bring his wife and three sons across the border. Fernando, now ten months old, his mother, two brothers, an uncle, and three cousins made their first attempt at crossing the border. They were caught and the uncle spent the night in jail in Tijuana. With nowhere to go, Fernando and his family members waited all through the night outside the jail for his uncle's release the following morning. They reached the coyote again, and he helped them. This time they made it across to be reunited with his father in El Monte.

So, in light of the sacrifices Fernando's parents made for him, they were rightfully disappointed in his actions, which disregarded those opportunities. It was a scary wake-up call for him that afternoon in 1994. He was taken to Juvenile Hall where he spent the night. The judge ordered him to serve two hundred hours of community service painting over and washing down many of the graffiti-defaced walls throughout the city.

Slowly he began to turn it around, and wrestling became a way for him to escape the tagging crew and criminal lifestyle. He spent more time wrestling and training. It was exciting to see him dedicate himself to the competition, considering his God-given talent. It was a special moment for me when the light came on for him; he had the potential to be a great wrestler. Fernando was another young man I introduced to FCA. I knew his family was Catholic, so he had the foundation of faith. It was just a matter of reintroducing him to that faith. He was diligent about attending the weekly Bible studies and attending the FCA summer camps. Somehow, he knew he needed that faith to keep him on the right path.

I then learned that his parents were moving out of their tiny apartment into a townhouse. The new home was in a city next to Santa Ana. Fernando's parents thought that it was too far away from Santa Ana High, and it looked as if he might not wrestle for the school. I was glad to see them moving out of a rough neighborhood, but it was one of those things a coach hates to hear, that one of his best prospects might leave the district.

A CIF (one of the primary responsibility of CIF is to administer high school athletic programs and enforce rules to a student's involvement in athletics regarding age, scholarships, residence, transfer status, and amateur standing) policy states that once students are enrolled at a school, they can remain enrolled, regardless of where they move. That policy was not an obstacle to him returning; however, the problem was that if he enrolled at his new school, the policy became defunct because of the transfer rules.

I tried to think of a way for Fernando to remain at Santa Ana and decided to make a deal with his parents. I would pick him up from school and drop him off every day after practice. Their acceptance was a huge relief for me but a sacrifice to me as a commuter; but there was the additional benefit of getting to know him much better because of the additional amount of time we spent in the car.

Toward the end of his sophomore year, Fernando improved enormously as a wrestler. He dedicated himself thoroughly to the sport, training at every opportunity and looking for every chance to compete. As a result, I got up at six a.m. every Saturday and drove him and a few of his teammates to special freestyle tournaments. He competed in about eight to twelve matches every weekend. It was amazing to see the focus he applied to the sport to become the best.

Coach Silva often gave speeches on becoming the finest, and he knew what he was talking about. He wrestled with the best and was among that wrestling elite at one point in his competitive career. Silva inspired the team to train like madmen, and his barrage of inspirational speeches took hold and began to reach them, especially Fernando.

In high school, Silva used to sneak into the wrestling room alone after practice for additional training. He would wedge a towel between the wrestling room door so he could sneak his way in against school rules. He drilled his moves alone in the wrestling room for hours. If he could not break his way inside the wrestling room, he would lock himself in his bathroom at home and drill endlessly. He drove countless hours to compete in any wrestling tournament he could find. Wrestling became everything.

With Silva's help, I did all I could to get those messages of dedication and discipline across to the students. It was great to see Fernando buying into it wholeheartedly. With his enthusiasm and commitment, it did not take long for him to become one of the premiere wrestlers in the area. Going into his junior year, he was a returning league champion but still somewhat unknown.

When he was a sophomore he wrestled at 103 pounds. Unfortunately, he failed to make weight at the CIF Sectionals and lost the chance to qualify for the state championships. Fernando had something to prove as that disappointment lit his fuse. Now as a junior at the CIF tournament, he waited to weigh in. There were a bunch of other wrestlers behind him, talking smack as they do. They were more than ready to remind him of his failure to make weight the previous year and give him heat about it.

"Who's this kid?"

"Fernando."

"That's him? He's smaller than I thought he would be," a wise-cracking kid said.

Fernando was more than ready to send the heat right back to them with skill, perseverance, and a little luck to take their championship titles. He came in at 119 pounds, wrestled with the best, and emerged a CIF champion. He might have competed better at about 112 pounds, but there was already a strong wrestler on our team at that weight. However, he held his own and had a great season, even though he was the smallest wrestler at 119 pounds.

It was good to see him continue to train throughout the summer and compete in freestyle tournaments. He was on a mission to place in state as he improved week by week. He put in two more seasons worth of training that summer.

As his senior year began, Fernando was in a position to excel, but his toughest opponent that year was not anyone on the mat. He became a target, and kids wanted to fight him. One in particular was a jealous, insecure punk of a basketball player who chased him around, pushing him at every opportunity. During a team run, Fernando accidentally ran into the basketball player, and he took it personally and enticed him into fighting on an almost daily basis, but Fernando resisted the antagonism and challenge because he did not want to get kicked off the wrestling team or suspended from school. Competing meant more to him than his pride. Though his final season had its difficulties, he did not get as discouraged as many of my other athletes. He knew how to bounce back from his setbacks and recover his focus and momentum, which was a credit to his strength and mental toughness.

I stress to all the wrestlers that it is nice to start out well and win during the course of the year, but how they *finish* a season is what makes all the difference. I have seen many wrestlers win all the major tournaments throughout the year only to fold up shop as the postseason championship events arrive. "Peaking" a wrestler, or any athlete for that matter, is one of the most complicated challenges a coach could have. My goal, as a coach, is to get each one of my wrestlers to compete at his very best during the last three weeks of the season. For the wrestler to achieve victory at the right moment, he must align the proper training regimen with a suitable nutritional plan, and most importantly, be free from serious injury. Fernando resisted that urge to stumble at the finish line and finished strong. He won his third league title and became CIF champion for the second time—the first two-time CIF champion in Santa Ana High School's history.

Then it was on to the Masters Meet, probably one of the toughest non-state tournaments in the nation. The meet draws the best for an afternoon of agony from more than 490 high schools. Many dreams come true, and many hopes crash that day. One can feel the intensity throughout the gym as coaches push their wrestlers to qualify for the State Championship Tournament; families root the boys on from the stands.

Eight athletes go on to the State Championships from the Masters Meet, with only one state champion in the various weight classes, as California does not have divisions. More than seven hundred high schools draw into the state championships. Hence being a state qualifier is a huge achievement.

Being a one-day tournament is the toughest part of the Masters Meet. Athletes can wrestle as many as six times in a single day. Weigh-ins start at seven in the morning, and competition begins immediately afterward—lasting all day. The competition is demanding for any athlete, but especially for the athlete who had to cut weight during the week while training and now must step on the mat.

It is a struggle to replenish lost fluids and nutrients following the weigh-in. Some of the best wrestlers in the state break down and lose. Those who did not have to cut weight too hard during the week could catch some superior athletes by surprise because they are stronger than their rivals. Since the tournament is single elimination until the semifinal round, one stumble and an athlete goes home unless the wrestler who beat him made it to the semi-finals. Then that wrestler has the opportunity to wrestle his way back into the tournament field with a chance to qualify for state.

The CIF did not make it easy for Fernando or any other dedicated athlete to make it into the state championships. At the onset of the tournament, Fernando came prepared to wrestle. He dominated the competition and made me proud when he found himself in the Masters Meet finals. He became the second wrestler in the history of Santa Ana Wrestling to make it into the Masters Title match. Fernando would face another Orange County wrestler that beat him earlier in the season. With the gnawing ache in my stomach, the fear of losing, and the dream of winning, I could only imagine how Fernando felt. None of the eyes in the arena were on me, but I could feel Fernando's agony if he lost—or his joy if he won.

He dominated his opponent that day. Our coaching staff was elated to have our first Masters Meet champion in the history of the school, a feat I never considered possible when I began coaching at Santa Ana. To have a *two-time* CIF champion and Masters Meet champion. Wow! He went on to the State Championships with the strength, skills, confidence, and experience to win it all.

Imagine our surprise then to see a different Fernando at state. No coaching class prepared me for some of the experiences that went with the job. Some of the biggest surprises came when an athlete had the potential to compete at the highest levels against top competition.

As Fernando prepared for just such a moment on the day of the state championships, I noticed he was all over his girlfriend in the stands before his match. The coaching staff believed that girlfriends were detrimental to a wrestler. Just as boxers avoid sex before a big fight, we believe dating and girlfriends lead to weakness. If an athlete is truly dedicated to his sport with a desire to be the best, he must realize that a relationship can prove a distraction and slow him down from reaching his dream, especially during a breakup, which always seems to happen right before a major match or meet. I went through enough of them myself to know that kind of emotional trauma before a major match is deadly. It will take an athlete out of the running in any competition.

Fernando was distracted at the state championship with his girlfriend seated on his lap. Fernando was also wearing new shoes, socks, and head gear. His entire wrestling ensemble had changed.

I am not one to be superstitious. Unlike one of my assistants, I did not believe I needed to sit on the same side of a gym to give my team a chance to win, but Fernando changing his gear seemed like bad karma, as he was not wearing the gear that got him to the big dance.

I had no doubt that he purchased it all to look cool because all eyes would be on the Masters Meet champion, but it was rare for any of the wrestlers to spend money on themselves like that. He won his first two matches at state unimpressively. He was not the Fernando I knew, and I struggled to find an answer as to why he was wrestling so differently. I simply could not understand his performance that day, and he lost in the quarterfinals. He could have won. He had what it took, but he did not come with the total focus he needed. Nevertheless, he had the next day to work his way back into the tournament's consolation bracket.

There are two weigh-ins at the state meet, one in the morning of the first day, and again that evening. Fernando did not eat anything that first day so that he would make weight that night at the second weigh-ins. He was worried, and it consumed his thought process. He wrestled flat because he was suffering from weight obsession. Wrestlers are constantly told to eat to replenish their energy level. Fernando let his obsession overwhelm that advice. He made the weight and was relieved enough to get a good night's sleep for the second day of competition and the loser's bracket.

He won his first match he needed in order to advance and place in state. That match was a barnburner because both athletes knew the loser was out; so they gave it everything they had. Fernando was thrown in a hip toss, a move that throws you from a standing position directly on your back for five points, but he recovered with an escape. In our program, we wrestle with the strategy of "take him down, let him up, take him down." The idea is to wear the opponent out to gain advantage.

Fernando used that strategy to catch up and pull ahead, but he fell victim to another hip toss late in the second period and fell behind again. In the third period, he returned to the "up and down" strategy to pull even. Finally, he pulled off a victory following a late period takedown. Relief flooded through us to have another state placer in the program.

It was pleasing to see him salvage something from the meet in a match that drew a lot of attention. It was the kind of confrontation a coach can walk away from with pride, because his wrestler came back twice to win. Fernando went on to place fifth at the state championships. What's more, the wrestler he beat for fifth place was the opponent who took him out in the quarterfinals (a little athletic revenge.)

After the season, the basketball bully continued to harass him, and he continued to maintain his composure. I was proud to see him walk away from this punk. He simply wanted to stay out of trouble and graduate on time. He did, and won the Athlete of the

Year Award from Santa Ana High School. That is a rare feat for a one-sport letterman like Fernando. That was a prestigious honor for him and our program.

A few months after graduation, he ran into the basketball player again at a mall. Once again, he gave Fernando a dirty, menacing look. Finally fed up, Fernando called him out to the parking lot and did not waste any time putting his wrestling skills to work. He put the guy on the pavement with a double leg takedown and told him not to get up, but the fool did and came at him. Fernando threw him with an arm toss back on the deck. This time, the bully hit his skull hard and split it wide open. The mall security broke them up, and the bully could only whine, "He had to use his wussy wrestling moves on me!" Fernando unpacked the appropriate reply: "Well, those wussy wrestling moves just got done kicking your butt!"

Of course, I do not condone or encourage athletes to fight. I think they are better men if they walk away. However, in this case, Fernando had to do what he had to do to deal with an unrelenting bully. He got the message across the only way he could. He never had another problem with him after that.

Fernando went on to wrestle at the junior college level, placing third in state his first year and winning the state championship meet his second season. Later, he took a job as a sales representative for an Orange County software firm and continued his college education part-time. He also came to the wrestling room occasionally to help the program.

His collegiate wrestling led to a contact with a wrestling camp in Boston led by Carl Adams, renowned wrestling coach at Boston University, where Santa Ana High standout José Leon wrestled under scholarship. Fernando spent two seasons coaching and mentoring wrestlers at Adams' camp. Carl was impressed with his knowledge and enthusiasm for the sport, so much that he invited him to become an assistant coach for Boston University.

Fernando would be coaching José and helping prepare him for the NCAA championships as a workout partner.

When the news of this lifetime opportunity was received, the delight was unimaginable. Fernando would be coaching at a Division I school, and I could not think of a better future for him. I was worried though, that he might turn down the opportunity because he really loved Santa Ana. He surprised me yet again by taking the offer.

After a year of coaching there, he returned to Santa Ana, sharing his experiences, adventures, and expertise with the new athletes in my program. I found him a part-time job at Santa Ana High and brought him on board with the team as the assistant wrestling coach. After three years of coaching with the Saints, Fernando found a higher-paying job as a sales rep for Wrestling Mart, a company that sells wrestling gear and attire. It was a perfect fit for him. Fernando still coaches the Santa Ana boys in his spare time. He is great at coaching because he can see himself in many of the young newcomers, and he has a true passion for showing them how the sport of wrestling can change their lives. The rat had come a long way.

Reflections on Fernando

Fernando taught me something I had yet to see a kid do on my team—walk away from a life of trouble and crime and channel all his energy into wrestling. I had no doubt that Fernando was headed for a life in and out of Juvenile Hall. Thank God he proved me wrong. He renewed my belief that the sport of wrestling can transform lives. His life reminds me of the scripture Philippians 3:13–14, "But one thing I do: Forgetting what is behind and straining toward what is ahead, I press on toward the goal to win the prize for which God has called me heavenward in Christ Jesus" (NIV). I know now that all the present and future Rats can find hope in this sport.

FROILAN GONZALEZ

1994–1998

> What you lack in talent can be made up with desire, hustle, and giving 110 percent all the time.
>
> —Don Zimmer, former Major League Baseball coach

I believe wrestling saved Froilan too. The sport pulled him away from crime-filled streets and gangs which could have easily claimed his life. He was an odd boy who walked awkwardly, with a head much too large for his skinny frame. The other wrestlers nicknamed him "Crypt Keeper" because he looked a lot like the creature with the same name from the television show *Tales from the Crypt*. He was not particularly gifted; as a freshman, he struggled to win matches, but to no avail.

However, I was not one to give up on a kid, because some of my least naturally skilled athletes turned out to be successful competitors. Froilan had the same chance to succeed as anyone else. I refused to cut anyone off the team, letting the tough rigors of the sport weed out the lesser competitors.

Froilan had a great sense of humor, and he kept the team loose as a joker and the butt of many jokes. However, I feared that after a few beatings he would find his way back to the streets. Surprisingly, he stayed through the whippings, though he did not compete in any meets, as he was not academically eligible. However, his determination was evident, and he stayed involved with the squad.

I wanted him to succeed, but there was always the question of whether he would ever earn good enough grades to enter competitions, as they continued to be a significant obstacle. I decided to have him tested for learning disabilities, and he proved positive. This discovery alarmed me because as I wondered how many other children fell through the cracks because no one ever thought to test them.

Nevertheless, the school transferred him into a special education program that gave him a framework to follow and a proper method to judge his abilities and expectations. As a result, he became comfortable with himself, and his sense of humor emerged even more. One time Froilan booby trapped the wrestling room, propping a bucket of water that fell on top of the custodian when he went about his nightly duties.

Froilan also found a new confidence and began to improve in wrestling. He was developing real potential. However, he needed more help than I could provide alone, so I introduced him to FCA during a youth ministry meeting at California State University, Fullerton. It touched him, and he accepted a relationship with Jesus Christ.

With this newfound faith, athletic improvement, and classroom success, Froilan gained a few pounds, looked much healthier, and became a genuine asset to the team. He was confident and held his head up high around the school. He soon became a capable wrestler by the time his senior year rolled around.

During this time, Froilan was league champion and placed in the CIF Championships. From CIF, he went in to the arduous Masters Meet, where placing top eight there would qualify him for state. He came in with the dream of making it to that ultimate goal. Unfortunately, he chose the wrong restaurant for his breakfast and arrived at the gym late. His match was called into action moments before he arrived, and he had to compete on a full stomach and sudden stress as he faced one of the toughest wrestlers in the state.

He got off to a good start, but it soon faded as the food took hold, and by the second round, he was pinned, and his dream was over. It hurt to see a year's hard work lost due to a big breakfast and poor time management.

Thereafter, he became bitter and resentful toward all the staff members. I empathized with him. I never made it to the state tournament myself, and I understood his painful disappointment. Froilan did exactly what I did; he blamed everyone else but himself. Nevertheless, he eventually realized the failure was his fault. As an athlete, he should have been in the gym much earlier, focusing on his goal.

He continued to wrestle at the junior college level and was fairly successful, finishing fourth in the Junior College State Championships. He further went on to hold several assistant coaching jobs throughout the county, then head coach at a local high school. He had about twelve students in his program, which was about all he could handle as a young coach.

He still amuses me, as he has not lost his sense of humor and wears a T-shirt that reads, "How am I coaching? Call 1–800-RINGWORM." It is an inside joke because the ringworm malady seems to work its way through every wrestling program. It is a contagious fungus that can be passed on from one wrestler to another while competing, and it can spread rapidly to others if good personal hygiene is not practiced.

We have retained our friendship, which I appreciate. It is rewarding to see that a kid who was selling drugs eight years ago has matured to an educated young man that is giving something back to the community.

The following comes directly from Froilan. He was kind enough to provide me with an interview and gave me a special, first-person look into the difficult, often terrifying, home life and childhood of a Santa Ana Saint.

Froilan Gonzalez
In His Own Words

I was born in 1979 in Orange County, California; the youngest of three brothers. We all lived in a two-bedroom apartment on Walnut Street in Santa Ana. Walnut Street is lined with such apartments, and when I looked out the door, I saw nothing but wall-to-wall people every day. When I was young, I saw drugs being sold, gang violence, drinking, shootings—anything that has to do with the streets. So, my family was very strict with me. By the time I was in second grade, I knew what was going on outside our door. My folks would always tell me not to hang around with the people out there and to stay out of trouble.

There wasn't much the cops could do because there was so much crime around. Most of the people causing it were Mexican—a lot of them illegals. They had no papers, so they weren't afraid to go to prison. And, if they were deported, they'd just come back.

Playing in our yard, I would come across bloody syringes, burned out joints, and beer cans. All of this would go on around us twenty-four hours a day. I understood that drugs weren't good for you, but the dealers knew that we little kids were important for their business. They wanted to be our friends and to keep our mouths shut. So, they would give us money to stay on our good side. If we saw them dealing or using, they'd give us a buck and tell us to go away and keep it quiet.

In our beds at night, we would lie there and listen to the fights going on outside. Gang members would shout their calls back and forth to each other. We could hear women crying and screaming because they were getting beat up or attacked. Gun shots—sirens—all night long, until we didn't even hear it anymore.

When I was in fourth grade, walking to school, I turned a corner and looked up at a light pole to see a guy dangling by his neck—hanging from a rope. We didn't get scared, but we simply reacted to it as a novelty. When we got to school and told the teacher, she was crying and very upset that we had to see that. She called our parents, but what could they do about it? They couldn't make it go away or pretend as if we didn't see it. We later learned that the dead man was from a different gang on the wrong turf trying to buy drugs. The rival gang roughed him up and killed him as a warning to other gang members to stay away.

By the time I reached junior high, I was fully aware of the violent world around me. You were either in a gang, knew someone who was in a gang, or you wanted to get into a gang. If you wanted to be cool or fit in, you had to be in a gang—or you'd be beaten or get hassled. They'd take your lunch money, hit you for no reason, or otherwise harass you. If you were in a gang or had friends inside, no one messed with you because you had back up.

I had a cousin one year ahead of me in school who was a member of Golden West Street gang in Santa Ana. He was pretty well known and feared. Their rivals were F-Troop, and both gangs were pretty big. My cousin was very popular with the girls and pretty powerful for his age. I would see all that and want to be like him just to fit in with everyone. I started running with his gang, but I didn't really become one of them. I didn't talk like them. I didn't dress like them. I just wanted to be noticed.

After a while, it started to get to me. Girls started noticing me, but other gangs also started taking notice. I would see fights around me every day—two or three bloody mad dogs (group attacks.) It would start simply with a punch in the face for no apparent reason, and it would go from there. I felt I needed to belong somewhere just for protection.

To gain membership in a gang, you have to be "jumped in." A couple of guys would beat you up, and if you can stand the beating without crying or passing out, you were tough enough to be in a gang. They were always on me to go through that and constantly asked me if I was ready. I never answered them because, while I wanted to be in a gang, I knew it wasn't really right for me. Still, though I wasn't "jumped in," they let me hang with them anyway. When members of F-Troop chased me down and asked me if I was in a gang, I'd say no and they'd just back off. If I told my friends what F-Troop said or did, they would promise to take some action—to prove to me that they were my true friends (my real family.)

One day, walking home from school, two guys tried to jump me and I fought my way out of it. When I told my gang friends, they were happy for me—like I was becoming one of them.

Fortunately, I had other friends not in gangs. They were in sports at school. I would try to join in with them, but my grades always meant I was the first to be cut. I think I tried to join just about every sport I could, but I didn't make the teams. As high school rolled around, I still couldn't make a team.

I thought I'd be in trouble because my gang friends all went to a different high school, while members of the rival gangs went to Santa Ana. So, I was a little fish in a small pond. Gang rivals would come after me every day to threaten me. I told them I was never really in a gang, but it didn't matter. I told my folks I didn't want to go to school because I didn't like it, but the truth was I was afraid. I figured every day would finally be the day I got beat up.

My freshman year, I met one of my closest friends to this day, Rudy Ramirez. In first period math class, Rudy would always ask me:

"Why is it that every time a bell rings, you run out of class like you're real scared?"

I would make different excuses and never tell him that I was afraid of getting beat up. Still, he would know what I was really afraid of and would say, "If those guys still want to beat you up, I've got your back." He would help me out because we'd become friends outside of the gang.

Rudy was on the wrestling team, and I always thought that was pretty cool. When the day finally came and those gang members cornered me, Rudy was there. A gang member said, "If you want to end this, let's get it over with in the restroom." Rudy agreed and said I should settle it. Again, he'd have my back, if I needed help.

We took it to the restroom and exchanged a couple of shots to the face. Neither one of us knew how to fight, so it ended there. I told those gang kids not to mess with me, and I made sure to avoid them. That was the end of my stupid messing around with gangs.

I tried to go out for football, thinking that might be what I wanted to do to fit in at school. My folks bought me cleats, even though I knew nothing about football. I never played sports at any level before high school, but I dreamed of being a natural—a hero. Sadly, when it came to practice, I didn't know what to do. I did meet another good friend Joe. Neither one of us knew what was going on, so we became the two jokers on the team. I think I played a total of five minutes that whole season, and we won just one game... by luck. It didn't matter in the end because my grades caught up with me again, and I ended up being cut.

Rudy knew I was disappointed about losing football, so he suggested I come with him to the wrestling room. I didn't really want to go, but I went along anyway. I saw a bunch of guys jumping all over the place, grabbing each other. I remember thinking, *This is gay*. It didn't look like I would fit in there, either.

Fortunately, I had an English teacher that really seemed to care about me—even though I was getting almost straight Fs. She talked to Coach Scott Glabb and told him that I needed some help. She thought wrestling might be good for me because I really didn't care about school. Maybe wrestling would give me some direction.

Coach Glabb chased me down as I was going out for cross-country in my latest attempt to catch on with some sport. He came down out of the bleachers calling for me. Coach talked to me about wrestling, training camps and other activities, including the Fellowship of Christian Athletes. I kept nodding my head, thinking there was no way I'd ever do any of this stuff. I just told him I'd try it... and the moment he turned his back, I flipped him off. I don't know why I did that, but he hadn't reached me yet.

A couple of days later, I finally wandered into the wrestling room and asked Coach Glabb exactly what I needed to do to be a part of the team. He said I needed shoes, the ability to keep my weight down, and earn a 2.0 average. Somehow, something inside me said, "Hey, maybe I can do this." Coach told me I looked like a natural and might be good at wrestling. That got me excited, and I thought I would belong right away. Popularity. Success.

But, none of that happened right away. I was the worst guy on the team. I'd gotten beat up every day, and the other wrestlers would tease me for being too skinny or weak. I tried to cover all that by just being funny and trying to fit in that way. Meanwhile, my parents thought I was crazy for joining the wrestling team, believing I had no idea what I was doing—just jumping from one activity to another. My parents just wanted me to get my grades up, but never wanted to help me otherwise. And, my brothers were too busy working to help.

When I needed money for new wrestling shoes, my parents couldn't help. So, I needed to come up with another way to get money. I never did drugs of any kind, but I knew where to find them and who sold them. The dealers knew I was an okay kid because I was never disrespectful or a rat. I learned how to sell drugs by watching the other dealers. I knew the prices of pot, crack, and everything else sold on the street. I knew the lingo you needed. You just had to get drugs, and the people would come to you.

So, a dealer gave me $60 worth of crack to sell. I sold it, and he kept $45. My customers were Mexican, black, white, and Asian. Some drove up in Mercedes dressed in suits, like doctors or lawyers with families. It would only take about 30 minutes to sell out to about 30 people. You might make as much as $500 in that time, but you had to stay on the lookout for police. The dealers all kept an eye out for each other. One call of "cops!" would send everybody running to stash the drugs. I was known around the neighborhood as a good kid, so it was easy for me to get away with it.

It was sad to see old friends from junior high showing up to buy drugs. They were skinny, their teeth shattered from the crack they smoked. One kid, who years prior, was a successful basketball player from Santa Ana High, came to me one day. He had gotten into drugs. Now, he was homeless, trying to scrape together enough money to buy a dime bag of crack. I noticed he was wearing a Santa Ana High School t-shirt. I felt sorry for him, and I gave him a couple of hits. He came back two days later, shaking and coming down. He grabbed me by the throat and wanted two more rocks. He wasn't asking me this time. He was telling me. I was scared, and just gave him some to stop him from hurting me. When he let go, I just ran away and kept an eye out for him from that point forward.

I figured out that, if I wouldn't have had to go to school, I probably could have made around $2,000 per day selling drugs. But, the fear of my parents eventually finding out that I sold drugs was urging me to stop. I didn't want to break their hearts with such a discovery. Also, a local cop figured out that I was probably dealing—though he never actually saw me doing it.

"If I ever do see you," he warned, "I will arrest you."

One afternoon, he did see me and yelled at me. I ran, and he pursued me on foot. We tore through the neighborhood, jumping fences and running through yards. I tried hiding out in different spots, just trying to avoid him. After a while, he gave up because he didn't catch me. I managed to lose him that time, but I was still scared. When I got home, I didn't want to leave the house to go to the store or even go to school.

About two or three days later, he chased me down in the alley behind our apartment. He didn't cuff me, but he threw me in back of his car and drove me around to a dead-end alley. There, he cuffed me and searched me. He pulled off my pants and dropped my boxers down to my ankles. I didn't have any drugs on me, but I thought this was all part of the search—until he tried fondling me. I asked him what he was doing and told him to stop. He got mad and just told me to shut up.

I don't know what would have happened, but he got a call on his radio to assist another officer. He pulled my pants back up and told me that if he ever saw me again, he would arrest me and something worse than that would happen.

I went on selling, but I was more careful. Even one guy pulling a gun on me and stealing all of my crack didn't stop me. I sold to women in Mercedes. If they were hot, I wouldn't want money. I'd have sex with them instead. One woman even took the time to talk to me and ask why I sold drugs. I didn't have a good answer besides wanting the money. She was a lawyer, and her husband was a dentist. Still, she had the addiction—even as her teeth changed color and she lost a lot of weight.

Finally, after about three months of dealing, I decided I wouldn't do it anymore. I would earn a thousand, and spend a thousand on clothes, food, and friends. After all of that dealing, I ended up flat broke anyway. I didn't even have enough to buy a little food for myself after wrestling practice. I remember trying to scrounge up a taco or two. My efforts failed and I was beat up by a couple of thugs hanging around the taco stand. I didn't think anything of it as I went home. But, I woke up the next morning too sore to wrestle or even walk. My ribs were broken. That put me out of wrestling for most of my freshman year.

One day, a line of police vans pulled up and hordes of police piled out. They arrested anyone who even looked like a drug dealer. They took in thirty guys that day, and I was lucky not to be one of them. It didn't take long for the drugs to return, but I wasn't selling them anymore. If I had, I know I wouldn't have finished school or remained on Coach Glabb's team. Staying in wrestling gave me more success than I would have found on the streets. I wasn't as successful as I had hoped to be in the sport. I was a CIF place winner in high school and placed fourth in the California Junior College State Championships. After junior college, I coached wrestling as an assistant at some of the local high schools and junior highs. I've got a good paying job now and was recently married. Life is good. My past has taught me to appreciate an honest job and how to reach out to others who are on the brink of making some of the same mistakes I did. I can now help them understand the importance of living a good honest lifestyle. A big lesson I learned throughout my wrestling career is that you can't mix dreams and goals with bad behavior. You will always come up short of the championship. Through wrestling I got to know the Lord Jesus Christ, got to graduate from H.S., wrestle in college, and get very good jobs. Wrestling taught me how to be a class act on and off the mat, and, most importantly, wrestling taught me how to be a man of character. I was one of many victims of a crime filled environment. I am not proud of my past, and I definitely don't blame my upbringing or anybody else. I am not ashamed to share my life openly now. My past is the reason for the person I am today. Growing up as a kid my mother always said to me, "No hay mal que por bien no venga." This means there is no bad that doesn't have a positive side to it.

Today I don't fear anything or anyone. The only fear I have is of God, because to fear God is to know him and love him.

My parents didn't have any education nor my grandparents. They didn't understand how to educate their children, but one thing they did have was a strong work ethic and they loved me unconditionally. My parents played the cards they were dealt with and didn't complain. I now have it much better than they did thanks to them. I appreciate my parents for working hard and giving me what I needed although they didn't have much. Thank you, Mom and Dad. I love you.

Reflections on Froilan

I have had several athletes walk into my wrestling room for the first time who were sloppy, awkward, weak, and uncoordinated wrestlers, and I thought to myself, *That kid doesn't have a chance of ever being a champion.* But Froilan reminded me that I shouldn't be so quick to judge those hopeless souls. I learned that a coach must have patience with athletes like Froilan and let their fortitude and willpower do the rest. Froilan, and the other wrestlers like him who followed, are a testament to all coaches that kids who lack talent on the mat may surprise you and shape themselves right into champions.

PHOTOS

First Team Championship @ San Clemente Rotary Tournament 1993

CIF DIV. III Tournament Team Champions 1996

Fellowship of Christian Athletes Wrestling Camp 1997

Paintball on team trip to Washington State 1997

CIF DIV. III Tournament Team Champions 1998

Coach Glabb Orange County Register Coach of the Year 1998

Orange County Summer League Champions 1998

Coach Glabb and Tony Perez High School National Champion @ 103 lbs. 1998

CIF DIV. III Dual Meet Champions 1999

3rd Place Team @ 5 Counties Invitational 1999

4th Place Team California State Championships 1999

Coach Glabb and Jose Leon High School National Champion @ 112lbs. 1999

Coach Glabb and Assistant Coach Joe Gonzales 1999

CIF Div. II Dual Meet Champions 2001

CIF Div. I Dual Meet Champions 2003

Assistant Coach Rick Lara and Coach Glabb 2003

Coach Scott Glabb Evergreen High School Wrestling 1980

FCA camp director Jose Campo and Coach Glabb 2005

Jose Leon wrestling in finals of high school nationals 1999

Gilbert Melendez Professional Fighter in MMA for Strikeforce 2008
Santa Ana HS Graduate class of 2000

Fernando Serratos (Masters Champ & 5th in State), Coach Glabb & Tony Perez (2nd State & National Champ) 1997

Jose Leon (National Champion), Tony Perez (National Champion) & Jose Najera (2nd & 5th in State) 1998

Glabb after Jose Leon wins National Championship 1999

Vince Silva assistant coach 1993-96 (All-American @ Oklahoma State)

Assistant Coaches Jose Morales and Sadie Morales 1997-2003

PHOTOS

First Team Championship @ San Clemente Rotary Tournament 1993

CIF DIV. III Tournament Team Champions 1996

Fellowship of Christian Athletes Wrestling Camp 1997

Paintball on team trip to Washington State 1997

CIF DIV. III Tournament Team Champions 1998

Coach Glabb Orange County Register Coach of the Year 1998

Orange County Summer League Champions 1998

Coach Glabb and Tony Perez High School National Champion @ 103 lbs. 1998

CIF DIV. III Dual Meet Champions 1999

3rd Place Team @ 5 Counties Invitational 1999

4th Place Team California State Championships 1999

Coach Glabb and Jose Leon High School National Champion @ 112lbs. 1999

Coach Glabb and Assistant Coach Joe Gonzales 1999

CIF Div. II Dual Meet Champions 2001

CIF Div. I Dual Meet Champions 2003

Assistant Coach Rick Lara and Coach Glabb 2003

Coach Scott Glabb Evergreen High School Wrestling 1980

FCA camp director Jose Campo and Coach Glabb 2005

Jose Leon wrestling in finals of high school nationals 1999

Gilbert Melendez Professional Fighter in MMA for Strikeforce 2008
Santa Ana HS Graduate class of 2000

Fernando Serratos (Masters Champ & 5th in State), Coach Glabb & Tony Perez (2nd State & National Champ) 1997

Jose Leon (National Champion), Tony Perez (National Champion) & Jose Najera (2nd & 5th in State) 1998

Glabb after Jose Leon wins National Championship 1999

Vince Silva assistant coach 1993-96 (All-American @ Oklahoma State)

Assistant Coaches Jose Morales and Sadie Morales 1997-2003

TONY PEREZ-BEAN

1994–1998

> History has demonstrated that the most notable winners usually encountered heartbreaking obstacles before they triumphed. They won because they refused to become discouraged by their defeats.
>
> —B.C. Forbes, (founder of Forbes magazine)

Tony and I met in the wrestling room one day after school. He was still a student at the local junior high. His PE teacher did a single unit on wrestling. At the end of the PE unit, the teacher organized a big match called the All-Stars. This is an event that is anticipated by the school staff and students. The best wrestlers from each PE period would square off against each other. Tony was preparing for this event when he first came to our offseason wrestling club.

Tony hoped to work out with our wrestlers to get ready for the event. One of the wrestlers took a look at him and nicknamed him "Bean." Considering his slight frame and skinny arms and legs, I suppose he did resemble a bean. Scrawny, lanky, and short, he did not fit the image of a wrestler, but as the saying goes, "Looks can be deceiving."

Tony was a much better wrestler than expected. He was decisive, skilled, and quick in his movements, very technically sound, a true student of the sport who learned swiftly and improved daily. A strong all-around athlete, he tried every sport in junior high, from cross-country and track to baseball, soccer, and basketball. He tried a little bit of everything, which improved his conditioning, coordination, strength, and dexterity.

Tony arrived in the U.S. when he was four years old from Pueblo, Mexico. His father had already lived here for a couple of years, working as a welder after being in construction, and had saved to bring his family over. Tony had not seen him for two years before his arrival. Accompanying him were his mother and grandfather. It took them three days to reach the border, and they had to hide in a truck during the crossover. His mother crammed herself behind the truck's seat while Tony pretended to be the coyote's young son as they snuck into America.

After crossing the border, the three travelers hiked up into the mountains on the other side of Tijuana, near San Diego. They camped out for one night in the cold, harsh mountains before facing the long trek across the desert to Orange County.

It is amazing how the prospect of a better life in America always outweighs the consequences of death, injury, or prosecution, should these immigrants not reach their destination. So many wrestlers faced that risk, as many of them came to the U.S. illegally as children. I thank God every day for the good fortune of being born an American, so that I, or any member of my family, would never have to face the perils of crossing the border.

When they arrived in Santa Ana, they moved into an apartment complex in a predominantly Mexican neighborhood. Tony lived with thirteen people (ten adults and three kids) packed into a one-bedroom apartment for a few months before moving on.

Tony's family moved quite often. They even rented a garage under a house in Tustin, using that as a two-bedroom residence for a while. Tony ended up sleeping on the floor for the first twelve years of his life in the U.S., going without birthday or Christmas presents throughout his childhood. His parents had five more kids after him, stretching their limited resources even further.

Tony attended an all-white school in the area, though he could not speak a word of English. He found another kid in his class who spoke Spanish, and they essentially used each other as translators to get through those school days.

With few options when it came to housing, Tony's family ended up moving into an apartment complex on Pine Street, which was then one of the roughest neighborhoods in all of Santa Ana, only a few blocks away from Santa Ana High School. It was a tough, violent area and heavily gang infested. Fortunately, I found that Tony never felt a desire or an obligation to join any gang. He hung out with many kids in the neighborhood who had older brothers within the deadly street gangs, so they offered him protection. He never had to do anything he did not want to do or face the risk of any gangs attacking him. Sadly, many of his childhood friends dropped out of school and got heavily involved in drugs. He revealed that he felt lucky that he did well in school, crediting Santa Ana Wrestling with saving him from his friends' fate.

After watching him work out as a junior high school student, I was immediately excited over the prospect of him joining the team. I was about to see Roger, a three-year varsity letterman who wrestled at 103 pounds, graduate. It is difficult to replace a 103-pound competitor of Roger's caliber; however, I believed Tony was the one wrestler who could do it. Other wrestling squads always envied our program's lightweight wrestlers like Tony, but we always had trouble filling the 171-pound weight class, and all the weight classes above. It is a hard fact that most Hispanic kids simply do not often grow that big. However, as Tony entered the program, we finally had some tough, competitive kids in those larger weight classes.

He had some experience under his belt, having competed in some freestyle tournaments before enrolling at Santa Ana. He had the mat time he needed to go varsity as a freshman, along with the necessary confidence to compete at that level. I thought it would be nice to fill Roger's big wrestling shoes with another talented kid at the lower weights. Tony was tough, and I felt confident that he would come in as a freshman and "hit the mat running," so to speak.

Indeed, he was exactly what any good wrestling team needed in a dual meet setting. It is essential to win that first match in such a contest to get the momentum of the overall match going in our direction. The Saints were always known for the lightweight wrestlers starting out the dual meets with top-class competition, and Tony fit that bill. With our first five or six weight class wrestlers winning, we could usually hold our own in the later, bigger classes and steal a victory. Tony would usually get out of the gate with a win, setting the tone for the rest of the squad.

By his freshman year, he learned to speak English fairly well, even as his family continued to struggle, mired in the forbidding atmosphere of Pine Street. Tony mentioned that his bikes were often stolen from his balcony, and his grandfather once entered their apartment to find a burglar at work. Fortunately, he was able to scare the thief off without incident, but it was obviously not the best of neighborhoods—a burden and a distraction for Tony.

In addition to wrestling, Tony embraced his all-round athletic nature and joined the cross-country team at Santa Ana. He would run in the fall and transition into wrestling, a winter sport, after cross-country took a hiatus for the year. The cross-country practice would end about four p.m., since all it usually included was a short period of stretching, warm-ups, and running. However, with wrestling, more was involved, forcing practice to run longer.

With the arrival of winter and shorter days, practice would often run into nightfall, so a freshman was walking home from school at night through a war zone of a neighborhood. That did not sit well with his parents, especially after his father was robbed one night while walking home from a night school class. His father said he wanted my lightweight star to quit wrestling to avoid walking home in the dark.

In truth, I believed the father wanted Tony home to help with the other five children. They clearly expected him to work or to get home after school and help around the house. He often said that his childhood was not the best of experiences. His father had a drinking problem, as did mine. He would come home drunk, raise hell, and throw tantrums—leaving a typical dysfunctional family in the wake. It left Tony apprehensive and reluctant to speak or stand up to his father. I was not sure how to resolve the issue of him quitting the team to please his folks.

Meanwhile, he was having a good freshman year wrestling at the varsity level. He placed in a couple tournaments, even while getting the constant pressure to quit from home. I finally sent Fermin Valencia and former Santa Ana wrestler Ronnie Ortega to speak to his family.

As a friend of the program and of Tony's family, Fermin seemed the perfect mediator. Tony had little contact with his father and he would otherwise have simply done what he was told and quit the team, wasting unlimited potential. Why not? It is common for some first-generation Hispanic families to pressure their kids to quit sports and work to support the family. It is a cultural practice that everyone needs to help in order to survive financially. Some wrestlers have told me that their parents think wrestling is a waste of time and that they will get nothing out of it. My hope is that these parents will discover the value of sports and education. I want them to have a little faith in their son's decision to participate in sports and believe the lessons he learns, the character it builds in him, and the doors that will open for him in his future endeavors are well worth the sacrifice of not making him quit something he needs.

Fermin and Ronnie convinced Tony's father to let him continue wrestling, on the condition that we find him a ride home after dark. I had done that before for others and had no problem doing it again for a good athlete like him.

He continued his strong freshman campaign, as coaches considered making a change. In some cases, athletes who train down to the next lower weight class can become even better wrestlers. The competition might not prove as stiff, and some wrestlers might feel they would do better one class below their natural weight. However, since Tony wrestled at the lowest possible legal weight, there was nowhere for him to go.

Rat, a veteran wrestler at 112 pounds, attempted to cut down to the 103-pound weight class. That nudged Tony out of the bottom slot, as Rat's superior strength and experience proved too much for him as a freshman. In addition, our best 119-pound wrestler, who often beat Rat, came down to fill the 112-pound slot.

Tony emerged from the shuffling discouraged because he was bumped from his spot despite some success, but, being the great student that he was, he understood that he had three years of competition ahead of him.

As a sophomore, Tony began the year by running on the cross-country junior varsity team, reclaimed his rightful spot on the varsity wrestling squad, and put together a tremendous season. He won a couple of major, prestigious tournaments and placed in the Five Counties Invitational, one of the toughest meets in the country. We were excited for him and had no doubt he would emerge as a state qualifier with the potential to place. In all my years of coaching, I never had a sophomore with such ability or so much success this early in a season.

Then fate played its role in his athletic life. He dislocated his elbow at the San Clemente Wrestling Invitational during the semifinal match. Though a common injury, it is extremely painful. His injury affected the whole team. We were making an overall run at the meet title before his injury, but his downfall seemed to set the entire squad back on its heels. There was fear in the air. The collective concern was "Could that happen to me?" That can often prove enough to rattle a team and take the fight out of them, but the Saints rallied on and wrestled for Tony, winning the tournament and dedicating it to their fallen teammate.

Two thoughts crossed my mind when I saw Tony's injury: one, he would not wrestle in the post-season, as his arm was unnaturally twisted, and two, his parents would have another reason to make him quit. As mentioned earlier, some of my athlete's parents look for excuses to dissuade their children from sports. His injury would be a prime excuse.

Another parent drove Tony to the hospital as an ambulance ride was out of the question. Like many other wrestlers, Tony was covered by the school's insurance. That, in effect, paid for absolutely nothing. If excessive medical bills were accrued, it would be additional ammunition for Tony's parents to insist he quit the program. Nevertheless, once he was treated, there were no assurances I could give that he would not be re-injured through wrestling again. Tony's parents were already at the hospital when I arrived, and Tony was looking and feeling better at that point as the doctor had already snapped his once ugly elbow back into place.

I was relieved to hear his parents were not planning to have him drop wrestling. It was a double burden off my shoulders. Tony was okay, and he would continue wrestling. My relief turned sour soon after, however, as I worried whether I could get him back on the mat with only three weeks left till the league finals. He needed to compete there in order to qualify for state. For many athletes, three weeks generally is never enough time to recover their strength and conditioning from an injury like Tony's.

I was amazed to find him back on the mat in just one week. We taped up his elbow very tightly, and he only drilled and conditioned, no live wrestling that might put too much stress on that tender elbow. I was very proud of my sophomore star, as most kids at sixteen would use such an injury as an excuse to avoid the rigors of competition, daily training, and further risk of injury. Still, Tony knew how important he was to the team and its first ever chance to win a CIF title. He pulled it together and wrestled at the league finals with one arm as his elbow limited his ambidextrous strength. We advanced to a shot at the CIF Southern Section Championships.

With only a week to go until CIF, I prayed for a miraculous, 100 percent recovery for him, but those prayers went by the wayside as his swelling and pain continued into the tournament. He wrestled with courage yet fell short of his goal to place in CIF. The young man that beat him that day went on to win the championship and placed in the state tournament. I came away very proud of Tony for his bravery and dedication, but I could only wonder what might have been if not for that elbow. On a positive note, our team went on to win its first CIF Wrestling Title in the history of the school.

Tony continued to train throughout the spring and summer. I was inspired by his perseverance and relentless training, despite the discouraging difficulties of his first two seasons as a varsity competitor. I have seen wrestlers with similar disappointments give up, refusing to step back on the mat or continue training. However, Tony never gave up, and his adversity only seemed to make him stronger. It gave him the will to become the best.

In his junior year, he quickly established himself as one of the best wrestlers in Southern California and perhaps the state. He was not yet the best in his weight class, but he was definitely a contender. His elbow problems were behind him, and he entered the postseason injury free. He placed third in the CIF sectionals and qualified for the grueling, one-day Masters Meet—the last step before state.

At the Masters Meet, his first match was against the experienced defending state champion. Imagine the team's frustration when we learned of his brutal draw, but I remained optimistic and firmly believed that he could find a way to beat the champion. We figured the champion would probably have to cut a lot of weight prior to weigh ins. That might leave him to step onto the mat fatigued and drained. Tony did not have the experience, but he had the conditioning, will, fortitude, and well-trained speed. There was an excellent chance to beat him.

It was the first match of the day, and Tony came out hard and fast, constantly moving and setting a brutal pace. He got out to a quick lead, leaving the champion weary. I believe his opponent lost before he ever stepped foot on the mat, and after the first round, I could sense that he knew what the unavoidable outcome would be. It was easily one of the best matches I ever watched Tony wrestle. With the crowd going nuts, he piled up a ten-point lead in the second round, essentially breaking his opponent, maintaining the constant pressure of "take him down, let him up, take him down, let him up." He broke him mentally and physically, leaving the defending state champion absolutely whipped. Tony got the toughest match of the tournament out of the way first, leaving a clear path through the Masters Meet. Indeed, he placed fourth and qualified for the state championships.

At state, he went in ranked tenth overall at 103 pounds. This was unlike any venue he had experienced thus far as a wrestler. The gymnasium is bigger than the rest, including a pit lined with eight wrestling mats below the stands, in which the wrestlers compete. A wrestler must wait in a tunnel leading to this pit, unable to see the crowd or the mat, intimidated by the roar of the largest crowd of the season. Tony obviously had seen nothing like this before, and his first match was against a higher-ranked wrestler, one of the best in the entire tournament. He got behind by five points early but ground his opponent down, eventually winning the match in overtime. He provided the biggest upset of the tournament and turned all eyes to him. Suddenly, everyone was rooting for this little underdog from Santa Ana High.

Tony fought through two more matches, putting himself in the semifinals. Once again, he faced one of the best wrestlers in the state. Using that same grinding strategy and feeding off his newly found crowd support, he scored yet another upset and earned himself a spot in the state championship finals, an amazing accomplishment for a student who, a year before, wrestled in injured anonymity. Now seven thousand people would watch a scrawny kid nicknamed Bean fight for one of the most prestigious state titles in the U.S.

Unfortunately, the odds caught up with him, and he was beaten soundly in the finals. However, we came back from the event proud of his accomplishment and progress. We all knew that the word was finally out that the Saints of Santa Ana were a team to be reckoned with, respected, and followed.

With the dawn of Tony's senior year, when he was still wrestling at 103 pounds, there came a change in him. It is easy to wrestle all out when you are the underdog no one knows, but with success, there often comes pressure. Suddenly, there is something to lose. Tony no longer wrestled without fear. He seemed to hold back a little, wrestling cautiously, as if afraid to lose. Going into the season ranked number one in the state, he wrestled too tight and seemed to struggle under the pressure. Expectations mounted, and he stumbled early in the season to an unknown wrestler. This time, he was the favorite upset by the faceless upstart. Up and coming wrestlers always want a shot at the best, and it is often tougher to compete with a target on your back against others who are hungry for your glory. The best do not always know what they are up against, and it is easy to underestimate the competition until it is too late.

Tony had more losses than we ever anticipated, even losing to a freshman phenom, and one of the best underclassmen in the nation. Tony knew he had to bounce back and wrestle harder to recover. To his credit, he never let his previous success make him lazy, and he continued to train in hope of righting the ship.

With the arrival of the postseason, he was no longer the favorite. The year before he proved himself as the second best wrestler in the state. Moreover, he began this year at the top. Rumor had it that his junior success was a fluke—a one-hit wonder. At the Masters Meet, he placed a hard-fought sixth, but still made it through to the State Championships.

By the time he reached state, most observers and friends believed he had lost his edge. They did not expect him to reach the finals. I knew then how Tony's first opponent the year prior must have felt, the defending state champion who fell to Tony in a first round upset. The battle on the mat took a backseat to the mental battle during a long, drawn-out season, and Tony was losing that mental battle. He still had the tools physically but somehow lost the edge. Throughout state, Tony wrestled valiantly but fell short of placing. I hurt tremendously because Tony was the last athlete in that arena who deserved to lose. I could not imagine what Tony was thinking and how he felt. It must have been agonizing, but he kept it together.

After state, there is a national high school championship tournament in which only seniors who once placed in the top two in state at some point in their high school career can qualify. Tony automatically qualified for the tourney at Duquesne University in Pittsburgh. We planned for him to attend nationals, following his junior year success. However, following his senior year struggles, I expected him to be too discouraged to pursue this competition. My gut told me he would not go for it after his failure at state, but when asked, without a blink, he accepted the challenge. He had indomitable spirit.

He began training immediately for nationals, while I had to begin fundraising to get him across the country for the tournament. The district would not be able to send him as it was not a state-sponsored event. I began a letter writing campaign to staff, faculty, and community leaders. We received an overwhelming response from everyone, raising thousands of dollars for him to pursue his dream.

As we boarded the plane for Pennsylvania, I only hoped that he would have some success at the tournament as he carried the hopes of everyone who pitched in to send him. He was ready and well trained, making the 103-pound weight class with no problem. He wrestled a great first match, pinning the three-time state champion from Oregon within a minute. It was as if his previous failures at state somehow lifted the burden of expectation and freed his ability to wrestle all-out again. Since he did not know the competition, and it did not know him, he felt no pressure. It was the old Tony, the one I remembered from a year prior.

He beat state champions from Wisconsin and New York and found himself in the semifinals against another California wrestler, someone he beat once and fell to once. The last time they had met, Tony lost, giving this opponent a psychological edge, but he was a different wrestler now and dominated his old foe. Some six minutes later, he was in the national finals. It was not supposed to happen. We had trouble coming to grips with it, but the opportunity was there, waiting for him to seize it—a national championship.

He would face another state champion, this time from North Carolina. The wrestler was undefeated with fifty-four straight wins during the last two seasons, a miniature bodybuilder who packed on extra weight following the weigh-in to give him an edge, but Tony would have to find a way to beat this bigger athlete to prove that he was not a fluke, to redeem his letdown at the state championships, to show them all.

I prayed for him, not just to a win, but also to remain injury free and to represent himself, the team, his family, his school, and his God with respect. When he walked out on the mat, I was proud to be in his corner. He showed overwhelming courage, looking like a twig next to the miniature Arnold Schwarzenegger he would wrestle. I did not know if Tony could survive this challenge since his opponent was so much bigger. Indeed, as the match began, Tony lacked the strength to offensively take down his challenger, and he had to alter his style. He became a defensive wrestler, scoring off his opponent's moves, including a couple of efficient escapes for points. Nothing fancy, just solid, controlled wrestling from both of them.

As the clock ticked on, I looked up to see the score, five to two in red's favor, and Tony wore the red anklet on the mat. So close, but too often I have seen wrestlers lead with seconds remaining only to get taken down or pinned late for a loss. You learn not to count the win until that last second ticks away. *Hold on, Tony. No mistakes... you are almost there... almost a miracle.*

A miracle it was as the buzzer sounded! In the final match of his high school career, Tony showed that he was the stuff of legend, a national champion who came from nowhere to beat the best that the entire country could muster. The night of the victory was a wonderful blur. It took a while for the truth to set in as the program had a national champion, and it would be known coast-to-coast in wrestling circles.

He became a bit of a celebrity after that, but you would never know from his unwavering, classy behavior. He won such a prestigious title and remained a humble young man. In fact, I recall that after returning from the tournament when his classmates asked how he liked the trip, he offered, "It was fine. I enjoyed it." When later asked why he did not share the news, he replied, "You never asked me."

I did all the talking for this ever-humble young man. It was great to see the school embrace him and better to see his father pat him on the back with pride as he admired his trophy; quite a transition for a man who wanted his son to quit wrestling four years earlier.

Tony was awarded athlete of the year at graduation and earned admission into California State University, Fullerton. He worked out with the Fullerton wrestling team during his sophomore year. By now he was weighing 118 pounds. However, the lowest weight class in the NCAA is 125 pounds. Tony was giving up too much weight and strength to wrestle at that weight class. Since he never gained the weight needed to wrestle 125 pounds, Tony decided to hang up his wrestling shoes and focus on his education.

He still visits the Santa Ana wrestling room on occasion and works out with the kids. He was also an assistant coach for a local Orange County team. He is one of those rare souls who can really have a positive effect on his community and young people's lives. He graduated with a degree in technology software programming from California State University, Fullerton. I urged him to pursue coaching, as he is an excellent teacher, and I hope he tries it one day. With his personality and work ethic, Tony makes a great role model for other young men.

As for the lives of other current Santa Ana Saints, they can look up at the wall of the wrestling room to a huge banner hanging there: Tony Perez—National Champion 103 pounds, 1998.

Reflections on Tony

Tony showed me what the words *determination* and *perseverance* really mean. His tenacity, his spirit, and his willingness to never give up no matter how bad he was losing was rare to see in a kid. I can't tell you how many times I saw Tony come from behind to win a match. Tony had heart—something you can't teach but every coach hopes his athletes have. If Tony could have that kind of determination and desire on the mat, then I as a coach should have the same when it comes to instructing and training these kids. Too many times I wanted to give up and let someone else do the coaching, but watching Tony gave me the strength of mind not to give up on the kids I coach.

JOSÉ LEON-ROCKET

1995–1999

> I think it's an honor to be a role model to one person, or maybe more than that. If you are given a chance to be a role model, I think you should always take it, because you can influence a person's life in a positive light, and that's what I want to do. That's what it's all about.
>
> —Tiger Woods, American professional golfer

Unlike many of my wrestlers, José was born in the U.S.A. However, when he was two years old, his family returned to Mexico, reversing the behavior of most of the wrestlers' families. Unfortunately, when they chose to return to the U.S. they had to do so illegally.

José was an American citizen; his parents did not enjoy that status, but they managed to sneak back into the country. As was the norm, José rode in the front seat with an aunt, while his parents hid underneath the back seat of the car.

He bounced around from one living situation to another. His

worst scenario was when his parents and six siblings lived in the bedroom of a house that also housed five other families. To make matters worse, illegal activities occurred constantly behind those walls, and José remembered constant gang and drug activities around him. Fortunately, he avoided any direct involvement with that destructive world, and his family eventually moved to Sixth Street in Santa Ana.

Sixth Street is a fair neighborhood these days but was another rough street to grow up on at that time. José told stories of drive-by shootings. His neighbors were gang members. He once got into a minor disagreement with one of them, and true to form for the animals in Southern California gangs they jumped him, beating him up pretty badly.

His parents stressed to their children the importance of staying out of trouble by telling them to mind their own business and keep their noses clean. As a result, José became withdrawn, and in elementary school, he did not participate in any extracurricular activities, including sports. After a day at grade school, he would go off to work with one of his parents, since there was no babysitter at home, and daycare was out of the question.

In junior high school, he had to return home to do the chores or to babysit one of his siblings. It was unfortunate, but as usual, some first-generation Mexican parents do not see the value of sports as part of the developmental process of a child's character. Hence, they do not encourage their children to try them.

José needed sports though—something to do after school. When he didn't accompany his parents to work, he would wander the streets, riding his bike. On one occasion, he was knocked off the bike and had it stolen outside a liquor store. Getting no aid after screaming for help, he tore after the thief, forcing him to peddle full speed. The thief did not know the limitations of José's bike—it had a loose chain that forced him to ride slowly. Of course, from the pressure, the chain tore off the gears, sending the culprit over the handlebars, knocking him silly. The bloodied loser limped away while José calmly replaced the chain and rode home. That was José, resourceful—a tough Santa Ana kid who made his own breaks—poetic justice.

Toward the end of his junior high days, he began experimenting with athletics, much to his parents' dismay. He tried football, track and field, soccer, cross-country, baseball, and wrestling. He tried everything and discovered he was good at everything—a natural. He stood only five feet, four inches, but he was stocky, solid, and well built. He was also smart enough to realize that he would need sports constantly to give his life some structure and meaning. The fact that he performed well in those sports spoke of his strong character.

As high school loomed for José, he took to wrestling when his junior high PE class did a unit on the sport. The four- to five-week unit taught the rules and moves. Some of the Santa Ana wrestlers and ex-wrestlers demonstrated techniques. Over the years, some of my best wrestlers came out of those PE classes. At the end of the unit, the PE teacher brought the best wrestlers together for a one-night tournament. For all of the students involved, it was the most anticipated event of the year, and the competitors took pride in their wrestling feats. The entire school turned out to watch.

The first time I saw José wrestle as a junior high athlete, he competed with a student who frequented the wrestling club to train. The young wrestler had some legitimate skills as a result, but José took just one minute to put the more experienced boy on his back for a pin. The entire coaching staff had a questioning look that asked, "Who the heck is that kid?" José was a natural, and everyone in the gym could see it. I could only hope that I would see him in the wrestling room a year later.

Entering high school, he tried football in the fall (where he earned the nickname "Rocket" for his remarkable speed and quickness on the field) and considered playing soccer in the winter, which was more popular among Hispanic students. However, once the football season wrapped up, he found his way to me, and it was the biggest blessing I could have asked for.

Too often, I found myself needing to sell kids on the sport. Santa Ana High is tucked inside a part of an area that is cursed with poverty. Families have very little money, and it is a sacrifice to cough up cash for athletic equipment. It is an uphill battle financially, as well as physically and emotionally, for any kid who walks into the wrestling room hoping to give it a shot. Fortunately, José had the God-given talent to pull him through all of that. I watched him step onto the mat and go eye to eye with sophomores and juniors, winning matches against older, stronger kids.

Nevertheless, I did not see the total dedication and killer instinct in him as a freshman. He was a part-timer, an athlete who wrestled only during the season, ending his training when the season came to a halt. He was still a good wrestler, and I hoped and prayed that he would find the passion to pursue the sport year round because I knew he could become one of the best.

During his sophomore year, he suffered a separated shoulder after a football game, but he transitioned immediately into wrestling, fighting through the pain. That earned him a spot on the varsity squad, and he had a tremendous campaign as a second-year wrestler. He fell short of his goal to place in CIF, but I was satisfied with his progress.

The program had two athletes place in the State Championships that year, including national champion Tony Perez. A few of the students accompanied the team to get a feel for state and watched their teammates from the stands. It helped them to visualize where they could be the following season. José watched Tony wrestle his way into the state finals, and that experience helped to change his thinking. He decided then that wrestling would become a full-time job because he wanted to be where Tony was, on the center mat at state before seven thousand screaming fans.

During the summer before his junior year, he began training on a yearlong regimen. He competed in freestyle tournaments every weekend through the spring. He and his teammates also attended various competitions weekly in a summer league that Orange County coaches formed for our high school wrestlers to participate. An ill-fated incident took place one evening as José and some of the wrestlers were traveling to a summer league competition. As they were sitting at a stoplight, some gang members in the car beside them started to "mad dog" the young athletes. Now, somebody who has grown up on any mean street across the country understands not to mad dog back at one who looks or acts like a "cholo" (gang banger), and my wrestlers were no exception. They looked the other way and avoided eye contact as they drove to the meet. Unfortunately, José had just made some unwanted friends. One of the cholos jumped out of his car at the next stoplight. In a flash, he ripped open the passenger side door, with knife in hand, and demanded that Erik (José's riding companion) hand over his 1998 CIF Championship ring. Erik knew the drill and, without hesitation, took the Ultrium-plated symbol of the team's success and reluctantly handed it over to the felon.

The next day I saw the boys at practice, and they were making fun of Erik,

"Coach, did you know Erik got married yesterday?"

"What?" I said in utter disbelief.

"Yeah, he married a cholo. Erik gave him his ring yesterday," they all said in unison, laughing and making light of something I thought to be very frightening and unbelievable. As I pressed them for more information, they explained the entire event and what took place with vivid details. I was angry at how brazen, yet full of bravado, these gang members were. I insisted to Erik that he and José file a police report. A week went by before I followed up with the guys about filing the report. They had not done it. I guess if one has not grown up on the streets of Santa Ana one does not understand how young people perceive being a crime victim. It seems to me that they take crimes committed against themselves with a grain of salt and are bothered very little by it. Of course, I think it is a front not to show their fear and is a way to cope with something that is inevitable. I told the two young men that I would take them down to the police station the next day and file the report.

Coincidence, fate, or luck you decide, but the day I was to take them to the station, I got a call from a police sergeant asking if I was Coach Glabb and if I had a wrestler on the team named Erik. Bewildered, I said yes. The sergeant went on to say, "We have Erik's ring down here at booking. We just arrested a gang member for murder, and he was wearing Erik's ring." I almost fell out of my chair when I heard the disturbing news. The sergeant asked me if Erik could come down and identify him and file a report, which he halfheartedly did. I could not fully comprehend the wrestler's near brush with death. The likelihood of them being that cholo's next homicide victim was a much-needed wake-up call for me. I understood that day the real hardships my wrestlers must endure on an almost daily basis to get to school in one piece and to live as much of a normal life as I do.

As José's junior year rolled around, he made the varsity football team, no easy feat for such a small person. The success on the gridiron did not stop his passion for wrestling. In addition to his endless training, he stayed on top of his studies so nothing would interfere with his quest to become a state champion. He was smart enough to know keeping up his academic effort would give him the opportunity to earn a college education through a wrestling scholarship.

He was on a mission that year, wrestling with mean intent. Coaches drool over wrestlers like José. Add a returning state place-winner Tony, and Fernando Serratos assisting in the wrestling room, and José had a strong support network to aid him.

He plowed his way through that junior year, winning the CIF title at 119 pounds and, placed fifth at the Masters Meet, eventually moving on to state. In the second round, he wrestled an incredible match against a returning state place-winner. No doubt that athlete thought he had the match won the moment he stepped out there, but José is an in-your-face wrestler. He never stops and keeps going until the match is won. That sort of pressure wears down opponents. José won that match on pure will and desire, thus instilling in him the confidence he needed to finish the tournament successfully.

He took seventh place at state that year and was happy with that performance, but I suspected he could have done better. Refusing to take a break, he was back on the mat the Monday afternoon after state, training for the spring and summer weekend meets. He knew he had one more year to get it right.

That drive was an inspiration to us on the team. José also excelled in the classroom, taking Advanced Placement (AP) college-level classes that included AP calculus, Honors English, and AP history. Somehow, when not breaking his back in the wrestling room, he found the time and the discipline to tackle a tough academic load, thus earning him scholar athlete of the year honors at graduation.

On the Saturdays he did not compete, he worked at his uncle's landscaping business and worked Sundays at McDonald's to pay for his wrestling gear. What fortitude. When I was in school, I tried working at Albertson's during the academic year but had to leave to focus on classes because I could not handle both. It is tough to balance. There was never a moment when José would sit down and take it easy. I felt he was a better man than I was.

Years later, I learned that José almost did not finish his junior year of school, nearly quitting due to personal problems. I believed sports helped him through that period, as it taught him not to give up and to fight through whatever opposition he faced. I can only imagine how awful this trouble must have been for a strong, dedicated student like him to consider quitting school and wrestling, the two things he loved.

About two years after he joined the squad, his parents offered to buy him a car if he quit wrestling. Essentially, they were tempting him with every adolescent male's dream, complete freedom of travel if he walked off the team. By then, it was not as if he was a fledgling, experimenting with the sport. He had been wrestling for two seasons with some success and dedicated himself to the sport. It was intriguing that they did not support him and revel in his success.

The automobile bribe was a tough one for a young boy, but to José's credit, he turned it down and elected to go on competing. His father told him he was wasting his time wrestling. José responded, "No, I am not. I am going to earn a scholarship and be the first person in this family to go to college."

Nevertheless, he entered his senior year excited and made the decision not to play football. For a two-year varsity letterman, this was a tough choice, but he wanted to focus on his wrestling goals. He knew that he had a shot for a wrestling scholarship, and that was his motivation for bearing down on his senior campaign.

He also spelled things out to his girlfriend, making his serious intentions very clear to her since she tried to talk him out of going to practice so they could spend time together. He put her on hold.

He trained hard, attended practice every day, and concentrated on his homework. It paid off, and he had a spectacular senior year. He made the finals of the Five Counties Invitational, a tournament that is ranked one of the toughest in the nation. José beat the number-one ranked wrestler in the state in the finals during a truly incredible overtime match. His success at Five Counties and a third place finish at the Reno Tournament of

Champions earned him High School All-American honors and gave him a lot of national attention. He focused then on a state title. If he could pull that off, he would hold the distinction of being Santa Ana High's only state wrestling champion, a feat not even national title holder Tony Perez could claim.

To get himself there, he relied on his favorite move: the fireman's carry, a quick, precise attack that throws his opponent directly to his back. He hit it multiple times on every opponent he wrestled, seeming almost unstoppable. As the postseason arrived, José won the league championship, his third in a row. He went into the CIF Championships, ranked number one in the 119-pound weight class, and emerged as champion again. He received Most Outstanding Wrestler honors and assisted the Saints in winning a CIF championship title.

At the Masters Meet, José cut a swathe through the field, only to face his nemesis, the same athlete he beat at the Five Counties invitational. They met twice before, and both had a win over each other. However, we felt confident that José could take him. This time his experienced opponent, who had started wrestling at a much earlier age, had all the tools necessary to score a mild upset, and José got beaten soundly. His rival was the better wrestler that day, but José pulled it together and ended up finishing third overall, thus qualifying for the state championships. It was still in reach.

He entered the State Wrestling Championships well prepared, and his early rounds at the tournament advanced easily. He made it to the semi-finals and prepared to face another athlete he had beaten previously. During the match, he made the slightest of mistakes, allowing his opponent a close upset win. José came up short in his scramble to make the state finals and emerged devastated. He was in shock, knowing that he would not have another shot to be a state champion.

I feared that his loss in the semi-finals would prove too great, leaving him unable to complete the tournament and salvage a third-place medal. I have seen this happen much too often, but José knew what he needed to do, as he realized third in state would still speak loudly to college recruiters. He hit the mat hard and secured a third-place finish easily. He was disappointed, but the High School Nationals in Pittsburgh still beckoned.

He began training for nationals immediately and decided to move down one weight class to 112 pounds, since the rules for this tournament allowed the competitor to drop a weight class if he chose to. That took a little out of him, but he trained hard over the month leading up to the event in Pittsburgh. With Tony winning a national title just a year before, José believed he could pull it off. Right on schedule, he whipped state champions from Oregon and Indiana en route to the national finals. Just one year after Tony's miracle at that same venue, José had a chance to redeem his state semifinal stumble.

He faced a tough, skilled opponent, the New Jersey two-time state title holder in the national finals, and after being scored on with a couple of takedowns and an escape, we found ourselves down five to two, going into the second period. José was however getting a feel for his opponent, and he used his signature fireman's carry to pull the match within two points. It was six to four, going into the third and final period. Those last minutes were a blur, with the New Jersey champion inching out to a seven-to-four lead. José scored a takedown to close it up seven to six, and then the referee awarded the tying point, calling José's opponent for stalling, delays in the on-mat action, usually to hold one's lead in the match.

I never saw the referee award that tying point because I was excited over the takedown. I thought José was still a point down. I thought he needed another takedown to tie and pull ahead, so I ordered José to let his man up. I looked up too late, realizing that José already scored a tie. By that point, the New Jersey champion got his escape on José's behalf and pulled ahead, eight to seven. With thirty seconds left, I had to make some decisions. Frustrated that I allowed him to let his man up for an eight-to-seven lead, I realized I would have preferred José to ride him out on the mat and take his chances in overtime. José had to take his man down one more time to win.

He managed to do just that but out of bounds for no score. With time running out, he had to chase his man down at the center of the mat before locking up again. His opponent blocked his move, maintaining his lead with less than ten seconds left. José lunged in for a front headlock and used all his strength, calling on all his hours of training and conditioning. He used a knee tap off the front headlock, a move he learned from assistant coach Joe Gonzales, the 1984 Olympian, and put the New Jersey state champion on his back for a two-point takedown and three-point near-fall. I watched the final seconds tick away as José became a national wrestling champion.

That match was easily the biggest and most exciting of my career. To see an athlete of José's character score such a dramatic win ranks as the highlight of my coaching experience. His opponent was only seconds from his national title, but José's fierce determination would not allow him to lose. He jumped into the air, running around the mat and pointing to the sky, saluting God for helping him reach his goal. He jumped into my arms, and we hugged in final celebration.

José, a kid from the mean streets of Santa Ana, a kid whose parents told him he was wasting his time, a kid who almost gave it all up just a year prior, a kid who is now the best wrestler in the country, was watched by every major college coach in the nation.

Not long after that match, he received a scholarship offer from Boston University. The staff there was not originally interested in him. Luckily, however, like some of the other wrestlers, he attended the FCA wrestling camp over a couple of summers, where they met the camp director and head coach of Mt. Carmel High School in San Diego, José Campo.

Coach Campo saw José's ability firsthand and realized his coaching friend at Boston would be interested in a tough kid like him. A phone call to Boston Coach Carl Adams mustered up a little interest, and when he saw José wrestle at the nationals, he was sold. Coach Adams was smart enough to snatch him up on the spot. It was a sharp move, because schools from across the country were calling for weeks after looking to give José a scholarship.

In his freshman year at Boston, José shot onto the wrestling scene quickly and had a great deal of success. He qualified to the NCAA tournament as a true freshman and was one of the top returning sophomores in the country the following season. Unfortunately, José had knee surgery during his final year of wrestling at Boston and was unable to get a medical red shirt to ensure him another year of competition. Therefore, he had to wrestle shortly after surgery with a knee that wasn't at full strength. Luckily, he qualified for the NCAA tournament for the fourth time but fell short of reaching his dream: All-American. It didn't surprise me that José would wrestle with such a debilitating injury. He is one not afraid to face a challenge. He has goals, and he refuses to shy away, no matter the odds.

José finished his bachelor's and master's degree in 2005 and completed his student teaching in Boston. I prayed daily that José would come back home to teach and coach. He did and now serves as a role model for the kids in Santa Ana, walking the halls as a living legend as a history teacher and my assistant wrestling coach. He had an offer to stay in Boston and teach, but returned home to give back to his community, a selfless act indeed, one only a hero can make. He continues to prove every day that a kid from the streets can make it all the way to college. He is a shining example of what any student from our school can achieve. My prayers were answered. On this note, I present an essay written by José Leon during his senior year in high school.

An Essay
By José Leon

Life is predictable, a routine, and at times, mundane. Highlights in one's life, though, make life worthwhile. Passions cause highlights in people's lives. Passions are enjoyed and many times are just hobbies that are relished during spare time. The world moves so fast that spare time is rare and is also all the time people usually have to enjoy themselves. This is why I feel it is important to pursue a career related to what impassions a person. High school has not just been an unforgettable experience for me, but has exposed me to different paths in the wilderness of life in the most perfect way. I have had great times as I have had bad times. Most importantly, I have been educated and have found a direction in which I will pursue in life.

During junior high school, I was able to handle the academics well while involved in extracurricular activities. After having gone through junior high school pretty much successfully, I was looking forward to high school in a very enthusiastic manner.

Having always been a sport fanatic, I made it an important part of my life. This passion that exists in my heart has made me strong and competitive every single day that I face life's realities. Ironically, sports is also a weakness I have learned to recognize.

I first participated in athletics in eighth grade, at junior high school. I played soccer, basketball, ran track, and wrestled. Soon, I realized that it was impossible for me to perform superbly in school while playing so many sports. I gave up all of them except football and wrestling. Up until my junior year in high school, I was able to keep my life balanced academically and sportswise. During my senior year, I discovered that I really loved the sport of wrestling, so I stopped playing football to become a full-time wrestler.

The discipline I learned and endured during hard practices, close matches, cutting weight, and an endless season has helped me get through some difficult times. By the end of my junior year, I faced some difficult and depressing problems. I was just about to drop out of school to obtain a full-time job. This happened during wrestling season, and if there are two things wrestling taught me, it is not to give up and to overcome with persistence. This I did and I thank God that I stayed in school. Not only has wrestling kept me in school, but it has given me the opportunity to take advantage of a free education at the university level. I have been given a full ride at Boston University and all I have to do is study and wrestle.

Wrestling has helped me and God has enabled me with a gift. I am thankful for this, but I know wrestling alone will not make me a successful person. I am afraid that my desires to become a champion will affect my schooling. I am afraid that my priority of receiving a college education will be replaced by a desire to wrestle. I tend to fall behind in my schoolwork during wrestling season. It is true that wrestling has gotten me a long way in life and has made me successful, but I also face an internal problem with wrestling. I love it. When a person truly loves something or someone, he or she becomes addicted to that love. This is my problem and I just hope that my aims will be accomplished.

The reason I love wrestling so much is because of a moment in my wrestling career that is one of the best highlights in my life. That moment was when I won the national title in wrestling at the 112-pound weight class was an indescribable moment with mixed emotions of joy, triumph, and relief. I would almost do anything to feel like that once again.

Another passion of mine had been mathematics. As a result of this passion, I have excelled in this subject. Right up to the end of my sophomore year, I had not experienced a lower grade than A, including time in summer school. Unfortunately, it is a passion I have lost for the moment because of an experience I had over the past two years with my math teacher.

My math teacher commented to me that, "Athletes get so much recognition that they do not deserve." Ever since, I have had a personal problem with her. I resented her remarks, but I did not react or rebel with attitude; this seemed to make our problems worse. As a result, I have not enjoyed math like I once did. Before this incident, I spent countless hours doing my math homework. Whenever I solved a difficult problem, I left triumphant and felt somehow invincible. This feeling in return made me feel good about myself because I would earn good grades. It might be my lack of creativeness that made me love the subject of math so much. I am not a mathematics genius, but I am always working on math problems. I also took an AP calculus test that left me very optimistic and I expect to regain that passion once more. I will not blame anybody but myself. I will move on, and after this nightmare, I will excel once again.

My passions have given me a wrestling scholarship to attend Boston University where I plan to receive a teaching credential and a master's degree. I believe I would be a very happy person if I continued to work with math while still being involved with wrestling. This is why I hope to become a math teacher and wrestling coach.

Everything I hope to do and become I obtained from Santa Ana High School, and this is also why I want to return to Santa Ana to teach and coach. A very big influence in this decision and my life is due to wrestling coach and teacher Scott Glabb. He is not just a teacher and coach, but he is a friend that I can count on. He is a big reason that I want to become a teacher and a coach, because I hope to very much be like this man.

Those are my dreams, to become a teacher and coach. I owe thanks to many of the personnel at Santa Ana High School as I see many of my aspirations becoming a reality in the very near future.

Reflections on José

José is a coach's dream, a boy who rose above adversity to win a national championship, graduate high school with honors, and earn a master's degree from a prestigious university. His accomplishments helped me realize that what sometimes seems impossible for my young wrestlers is possible. He is a role model for all the kids in the program. His life gives me a story to share with those wrestlers who have followed behind him and who question their hope that it can be done. José's national championship banner hangs on one side of the wrestling room as a symbol of the ambition, courage, and desire it will take to be a success on and off the mat. I point to his banner daily—or him if he is the wrestling room—as I try to motivate my wrestlers to be the same.

THE UNSUNG HEROES

This section is dedicated to those wrestlers who did not get the public and media recognition they deserved, but who did all of the right things during their high school wrestling career. They showed up for practice, got the grades, and put in the effort to be successful. Maybe they did not have it as hard as many of the other wrestlers, but they were not spoiled either. They were able to stay focused and out of trouble in Santa Ana. It would not be right to forget these athletes.

Society places special recognition on the young people who rose from adversity to achieve. I paid special attention to them on the aforementioned pages, but there is much to be said about other student athletes who never suffered or caused any problems and helped to build the program into what it is today. I could always count on them, and I always will.

Unsung Hero—Alonzo Ramirez
A Born Leader
1990–1993

During my first season as coach of the Saints, I looked around the wrestling room searching for an athlete. I sought a superstar, that one special kid that could give me hope and a reason to keep fighting through the difficult year. As it turned out, he was not in the wrestling room but on the football field.

Alonzo was the best wrestler I could hope for at that time. He was a sophomore, but I looked to him for leadership and success and built the program around him. Though only a second-year wrestler, he had the necessary athleticism, and he was my only hope to build a foundation to start the program.

At six feet tall, broad shouldered, and bowlegged, he stood out among the other students at Santa Ana. He also wore a half-moustache, the kind of facial hair only a teen could grow. However, he was one of the better amateur wrestlers early in his training, and, more importantly, he had the leadership qualities I sought, which was unusual as I encountered only a handful who rose to the challenge of becoming a leader in the wrestling room. For some reason, it appears that many of the young men I work with do not embrace leadership. Perhaps they fear offending teammates or retribution, maybe even being mocked or laughed at. It is a sad fact that I have to deal with on the team.

Nevertheless, Alonzo was an exception. He was never afraid to lead because he came from a family of athletes, including a brother and sister who competed successfully at Santa Ana. He consistently maintained above average grades and was involved in student government. When not wrestling, he played football in the fall and ran track and field during the spring. He was a natural athlete with the confidence to lead. The only problem was his tendency to tell too many bad jokes, but the fact that he insisted on telling them was funny in itself. He wrestled at 171 pounds during his sophomore year, a weight class that, to my surprise, he never grew out of in the years to come. He was one of two wrestlers from the squad to qualify for the CIF Championships in my first season. Unfortunately, he failed to win a league title that year and the year to follow as well. However, in his senior year he took the title.

During his previous campaigns, he competed against one of the toughest wrestlers in state history, Tito Ortiz, who once held the title of UFC Light Heavyweight Champion. Ortiz pulverized Alonzo every time they met on the mat. Fortunately, Ortiz moved up a weight class, and Alonzo won the league championship in his final year.

Alonzo continued to exercise his leadership role and was a solid and helpful teammate. Later on in his tenure, his quick thinking saved what would have been a very embarrassing situation that occurred during a practice session with another athlete Carlos.

Carlos was an outstanding freshman varsity wrestler the previous year, but as a sophomore he lost interest in the sport and was only practicing because I begged him to come back out for the team after football season. During one practice, he lay winded at the side of the mat while the other guys were wrestling live, at full speed. He was out of shape and could not be bothered to pick himself up. I instructed a wrestler to get him out of the way, lest someone stumbled over him, causing injury. He was dragged by his feet out of the way, and he immediately took offense to his teammate's assistance. He then accused me of treating him like a dog. A verbal battle ensued, and I ordered him out of the room.

"You are treating me like a dog," he said, walking off into a corner, adding other expletives.

"I never treated you like a dog, and I never would, you big dummy," I retorted, catching myself too late.

My retort lit a fuse, and he charged at me as I stood in amazement, watching him approach me for a brawl. Alonzo immediately restrained him before he could reach me. I thanked him sincerely, as I do not know what the outcome would have been.

Carlos never returned to the wrestling room, but I was thankful to see Alonzo roll in every day. He had a tremendous senior year, finishing third at the Masters Meet (a great accomplishment), but then he broke his big toe one week before the State Championships and could not compete at 100 percent. He won only one match at the state meet. One of his opponents, whom he had earlier beaten in the season, had placed at the state meet. It is difficult to explain how frustrated an athlete feels when an opponent he had beaten previously now stands atop the podium while the brokenhearted athlete peers from the stands. Only athletes who have been in Alonzo's shoes can explain the agony one feels during that moment.

After high school graduation, Alonzo wrestled at the local junior college with success and then left for vocational school in Oklahoma to study airplane mechanics. With a vocational degree and his natural ability to lead, I have no doubt Alonzo will be a success in whatever endeavors he pursues. He visits occasionally, still looking in great shape, still sporting that cheesy moustache of his, and still telling his jokes. However, I must say they have gotten a little better.

Unsung Heroes—the Morales Brothers
Steadfast Commitment Times Two
1992–1996

Brothers Sadie and José Morales wrestled during a key period in the program's development, and they contributed more to it than any other alumni. Born in El Salvador, their mother immigrated to the U.S. before bringing the boys over in time to start their education. They received legal residency through political asylum. They did not know their father. Through this mother's dedication to her boys, however, they were well-adjusted children who did well at school and devoted their athletic years to wrestling. They are quality young men. I salute them, and their mother for beating the odds.

They were active in church and lived the life of faith earnestly. The brothers were also heavily involved in the campus ministry, Fellowship of Christian Athletes, attending their summer wrestling camp for several years. I had never encountered young men dedicated to living a just life until I met Sadie and José, and I rarely find men more trustworthy than these two brothers. There was always chaos on the team as I scrambled around dealing with the unusual challenges of an urban high school, but I could rely on Sadie and José during and after competitions.

Sadie joined as a freshman, bringing past experience from junior high school. José, who is a year younger, joined the following year. They had some natural talent. They took the sport seriously and lived the lifestyle necessary to be successful. They did not indulge in drinking, smoking, or drugs, nor did they chase girls. They were focused all year round, training and competing at every opportunity. They were fortunate to be under the tutelage of Coach Silva, my top assistant at the time, and their confidence grew, which elevated them to compete at the state level.

During their senior and junior year respectively, they competed for a southern section CIF title, and with them leading the way, Santa Ana brought home the first championship in the school's history. Sadie was a CIF champion and the first two-time state placewinner in the history of the school. He is one of only three athletes from the program to accomplish that feat. José was less accomplished, but no less dedicated. No one was happier than I that these two fine young men could be a part of that achievement.

Following graduation, Sadie joined the team as a coach, and so did José after gaining his diploma. Both coached for several years with the Saints before transferring to another school in the district, Santa Ana Valley. There, they worked with Frank Pinto, another Santa Ana High School alumnus, who teaches science and is also building a wrestling program that emulates that of his alma mater. Along with Frank, Sadie and José passed on the outstanding influential teachings of Coach Silva to their new team members. Their goal: to someday soon beat their former high school coach in a dual meet. Sadie is currently working for the United States Postal Service, and Joe is in management at IKEA.

Unsung Hero—Ignacio Bravo
Break 'Em and Take 'Em
1992–1996

We called him Nacho. I was filling in as a football coach for a season on the freshman squad and used the opportunity to recruit athletes into wrestling as I was desperately looking for bodies to fill my roster. I found Nacho when he was playing freshman football. He was a small kid, weighing about 110 pounds, who wore thick glasses that he was almost blind without. He had no business playing football.

Nacho was likable, possessing a soft side to his nature that distinguished him from the other athletes on the squad. He wore his heart on his sleeve and had a vulnerability about him that made it impossible not to be drawn to him. He arrived with his mother from Mexico at the age of three, never knowing his father.

His mother found a job as a cleaning woman, while Nacho sold oranges at a street corner, earning as much as three hundred dollars in a weekend. He lived in a neighborhood run by F-Troop, a dangerous Hispanic gang, but he avoided them and credits sports with keeping him on a straight path.

He maintained his character and discipline in school and during competitions, but he was tormented with the struggles of gaining citizenship. While he and his mother battled to get his immigration papers in order to gain total freedom, clerical errors and other problems continued to thwart him. When he turned twenty-one, he had to reapply, starting the nightmare all over again.

Throughout his personal struggles, Nacho found the strength to wrestle and the will necessary to resist quitting, a determination within him that I have not witnessed from any other wrestler. He never took breaks during workouts and was always the last athlete in the room when practice ended.

Refusing to tire or get frustrated during competition, he

became known for breaking his opponents by wearing them out. In one particular match, he trailed fourteen to two but refused to fade. His opponent ran out of gas, and he rallied back, scoring seventeen points by taking his opponent down and letting him up, then finally pinning him. Nacho was notorious for the "break 'em and take 'em" philosophy we taught to our team. If his opponent had more experience, Nacho made up for it with his conditioning and beat several of his competitors by his sure willpower and determination. As a coach, it was thrilling to watch how he mentally and physically wore his competition down.

He was emerging into a quality wrestler when his mother decided to move to Georgia, as she sought a better job opportunity. Nacho moved in with his brother, who gained guardianship of him. He lived on the back porch between four hastily built temporary walls. Though upset and hurt that his mother left, this did not break his spirit, and he continued wrestling throughout his senior year. He won the CIF championship and became the first wrestler in Santa Ana High School's history to wrestle in the Masters Meet Finals. He took seventh place in the State Championships that year but desperately wanted to win it all and believed he could. I watched him sob with disappointment as he watched the kid he beat for the CIF Championship place first in State. . I was immensely proud of him, and in my heart, I believe he deserved to win, but it was not to be—despite his unquestionable dedication.

It grieved me that Nacho was unable to attend college because of his non-citizen status. Without a social security number, he managed to secure an INS work permit, and my sister, who always liked his kind demeanor, reached out and provided him with a job at her software duplication company. After working for my sister for seven years, Nacho moved to Atlanta, Georgia, to be closer to his mother. Nacho is a special young man who deserves better than what came his way.

Unsung Hero—Gilbert Melendez
Mental Toughness
1997–2000

There are times when a coach encounters an athlete he wishes he could clone ten times over; in fact, he wishes the entire team were clones of this one athlete. Gilbert Melendez was such an athlete. I first saw Gilbert as a junior high competitor, wrestling at a local intramural meet, and I was hoping he would attend our school. His father was usually a spectator, which was a rarity in Santa Ana. Most parents do not usually attend such events. Mr. Melendez was friendly and introduced himself one day, with Gilbert at his side. There was genuine respect and class in both of them. It was obvious that Gilbert had the potential to be a champion.

They lived conveniently a few blocks away from Santa Ana High, so I thought I could enjoy seeing Gilbert wrestle on the team. I soon found out that he was scheduled to attend another high school in the same district, even though his parents graduated from Santa Ana. It looked as if he would be an opponent.

Gilbert attended the other school during his freshman year, but unfortunately, his first year of high school wrestling was somewhat of a disappointment, and he wanted to attend Santa Ana High to wrestle. It was a great compliment to our program, and it was a first for me to meet a young student who actually wanted to attend a rough and tough school to wrestle. Fortunately for the both of us, Gilbert's father supported his son's love of wrestling and, of course, wanted to see him excel. With his parents' blessings, Gilbert enrolled at Santa Ana High.

Due to district transfer rules, he was unable to compete at the varsity level, but he spent his sophomore year training with seasoned champions like José Leon, who assisted in his development. He was full of fortitude, fight, and had the drive necessary to succeed, rare qualities not often seen in young kids.

Consequently, he had a successful junior year. He looked forward to a spectacular final campaign and sailed through his senior year especially, as he was ranked as one of the top four wrestlers in the state at his weight. It was exciting to watch him wrestle, and I felt confident that he would place in state for Santa Ana High.

Tragically, he broke his elbow during warm-ups before league finals but kept on fighting, for fear of his dream being taken away. He wrapped his elbow up, wrestled, and won the league title. He kept his suffering to himself. When the team finally found out the extent of his injury and that he would need surgery we were all shocked. It was grossly unfair. He asked his orthopedic surgeon if he could wrestle the last three weeks of the season and then get surgery With bewilderment the doctor said yes. With a heavily padded elbow and gruesome pain, Gilbert competed in his postseason qualifying tournaments. He placed second in the CIF Championship, which qualified him to the Masters Meet. There he finished sixth, qualifying for the State Championships. It was the most inspirational sight, seeing him wrestle with one arm.

In the first round of the state meet, Gilbert drew one of the top ranked wrestlers in the state, and with guts and fortitude still intact, he beat his opponent; but that was when the pain and fatigue finally kicked in, and he lost the final two matches of his high school career. He walked off the mat like a man, with a stoic countenance and his head held high. Once out of spectators' view, he collapsed into his father's arms and cried. I felt his pain. Gilbert did not place at state as we had all hoped, but he contributed much more to the program than he will ever know.

His story endures to this day. I use his experience as a benchmark for guts, determination, courage, and dedication when wrestlers complain about pain or fatigue during practice. No doubt, Gilbert Melendez wrestling with a broken elbow will be told in the wrestling room for years to come.

He underwent surgery to repair his elbow and moved on

to wrestle at San Francisco State for a few years. He gradually became disheartened with his college wrestling team. They did not have the same work ethic as the Santa Ana wrestlers. He tried his hand at mixed martial arts (MMA), a full-contact combat sport that allows a wide mixture of fighting styles. With Gilbert's aggressive style of fighting, he shot up through the rankings rather quickly. He is now one of the most accomplished MMA fighters in the world. As a coach, I couldn't be prouder. He is one of the first professional athletes that have come out of Santa Ana High School for the past two decades. A couple of times a year he stops by the wrestling room to work out with the team and share his story. He encourages our young wrestlers to dream big, work hard, and never forget where they came from: Santa Ana.

Unsung Hero—Alex Becerra
Risk Taker
1996–2000

Apart from fundraising, recruiting is one of the toughest jobs for a coach. It was a bane in my side to fill the higher weight classes on my roster because I was primarily dealing with physically smaller Hispanic students, which made it tough to win dual meets. Alex Becerra changed that.

Alex was born in the United States and was the son of a Hispanic father and Caucasian mother. He had two younger siblings. Their lives spiraled downhill when their parents divorced and his father took them back to Mexico. His father remarried and had four more children, three boys and a girl, and when Alex was ready to attend sixth grade, his father, stepmother, and the seven children returned to the U.S., where they lived in a two-bedroom apartment.

Alex was by no means huge, but much bigger than many other students, and I do not often see many of his build. He had the physique of a wrestler; he looked tough and would be capable enough to fill the upper weight class. Alex was enrolled in my freshman English class, where I spoke to him about wresting daily. He was not immediately interested in the sport, but I continuously invited him to come on board. He eventually succumbed to the risk and accepted the challenge, perhaps to escape his less-than-comfortable living conditions. Often young athletes feel with the risk of going out for wrestling will come defeat, thus to save face they avoid trying out or competing at all.

He had the strength and quickness necessary, and with mat time, he caught on to the sport with zest. He never missed practice, complained, or shrugged off a challenge. He regularly won and placed in tournaments locally, always giving his absolute best effort during competitions. He stayed the course, was a two-time CIF champion, and placed a respectable third in the State Championships.

His two younger brothers later joined the team, which was an added bonus. Jimmy Becerra placed fifth in state, while Scott Becerra, though not a state place-winner, contributed to the squad tremendously. Not surprisingly, the name Becerra has become fairly well known throughout California as quality wrestlers. After high school, Alex and Jimmy wrestled at the local junior college were their success continued. Alex placed third at 275 pounds in the Junior College State Championships, while his brother Jimmy placed second at 197 pounds. Their accomplishments at the junior college level earned them both scholarships to N.A.I.A. (National Association of Intercollegiate Athletics) college in the Midwest. I was shocked to hear that the brothers accepted the offer, for it is uncommon, in my experience, that a Santa Ana High School graduate travel halfway across the United States to attend college. Usually, Santa Ana kids put staying with family first. Therefore, few move out of the area to attend college. I am proud that the Becerra boys once again took a risk, stepped beyond their comfort zone, and challenged themselves to go to school afar. In fact, after a season of wrestling, the Becerra brothers emerged as N.A.I.A. All-Americans. Jimmy finished seventh, and Alex placed fifth at their respective weight classes.

Alex went on the following year to place second in the N.A.I.A. Championships. Alex accomplished a great deal in wrestling. I can still picture the look on his face as he sat in class when I asked him daily to take a chance and go out for wrestling. Throughout his career sometimes I wonder what life would have held for Alex and his brothers if Alex had never taken my advice to come out for wrestling. Though the Becerra's will end their wrestling careers as All-Americans, more importantly, they'll walk away with an education too.

Unsung Hero—Wyatt Howard
Cultural Differences
2000–2001

Even with the success I have accomplished in the wrestling program, there is always some measure of insecurity to deal with as I worry about what the administration, other coaches, and fans of the sport think of the Saints.

One of the greatest assurances and compliments I have ever received was when Wyatt Howard transferred from Irvine High School to Santa Ana High. Irvine is an upper-middle-class city in Orange County with predominantly white and Asian families. Irvine Unified School District is efficient and produces students with high test scores. It is a world apart from Santa Ana High, so imagine my glee and shock over Wyatt's transfer. Such a move was unheard of in Orange County, but apparently, during his junior year at Irvine, he and his dad differed with Wyatt's coach on training philosophies, and his parents decided to allow him to attend Santa Ana.

With his six-foot-two-inch frame, pale skin, and blonde hair, Wyatt stood out like a sore thumb amongst the more smaller statured students. He was relatively shy and was known to keep to himself when he attended Irvine High. Wyatt trained hard and adjusted well to his new surroundings. In fact, after practice one day, Wyatt returned to the locker room to discover that fifty dollars were stolen from his locker. He did not put a lock on his locker. He was used to leaving his locker unlocked at Irvine; he thought he could do the same at Santa Ana. Some of the guys responded to Wyatt's misfortune by saying, "Welcome to Santa Ana High School!" His new teammates looked at his financial loss as his initiation into in the program. It disappointed him to realize his own teammates would steal from him. The wrestlers knew being a victim of theft at our school was inevitable and would eventually happen to Wyatt sooner or later. His parents were supportive, embracing the wrestling program and their son's new school emotionally and financially. The Howards became an important family to the program, and I came to know them fairly well.

Due to young Wyatt, Santa Ana won their seventh CIF Championship, and he went on to place fourth in the State Championships in his senior year, also graduating at the top of his class. His success as a student and wrestler was no surprise to anyone who knew him, but his progress socially was astounding. Wyatt went from a kid who ate alone at lunchtime to a young man who danced with other students in a performance at a school-wide assembly. He even found a girlfriend by year's end. To say the least, I was pleased to see the miraculous change Wyatt made in one year of attending our school. It reinforced my confidence in Santa Ana High and sent a message to the community that our school had a great deal to offer any student from any socioeconomic background.

His transfer also sent a message that change can be a good thing. So many of us fear change. However, for Wyatt, a new school, new friends, and a new team brought out the best in him. I admire him for taking that step of faith and leaving everything he knew and was familiar with behind and walking into a whole different culture, unsure of his fate. Even though Wyatt was an exceptional wrestler and had a work ethic every college coach desires in a new recruit, he decided to give up wrestling and focus on his academics. He attended two years at a local junior college and transferred to UC Berkeley, graduating with a major in mathematics. His family remains involved with the program, endowing a foundation that once offered scholarship monies for Santa Ana wrestling graduates to attend college, and they also provided tutoring for wrestlers who needed assistance.

Wyatt and his family are a tremendous blessing to the program, always reaching out to the Saints unconditionally in helping them to get ahead, and I wholeheartedly thank them.

BUBBA–THE UNREDEEMABLE

1991–1995

> It's not that some people have will power and some don't. It's that some people are ready to change and others are not.
>
> —James Gordon, M.D. (Harvard educated psychiatrist)

Throughout my career at Santa Ana, I have touched the lives of many students through my work as a teacher and wrestling coach. Some took the opportunity to use the sport as a vehicle to further their education by way of scholarships, and others, to become decent members of society. Still others could not be saved or chose not to change.

One such student that is of particular interest is Bubba. Bubba was hanging out with the wrong crowd and found trouble around every corner. This got him kicked out of school in the sixth grade. As a result, his parents could not handle him and sent him to Mexico to live with his grandparents. There, he grew up fighting grown men at every opportune moment. He finally moved back to Santa Ana and returned to Santa Ana High School as a freshman, but Bubba still had some fight left in him.

No sooner was he back when he was caught fighting with other students, and his special education teacher took him to the wrestling room in the hope that wrestling would teach him discipline and help to change his attitude.

Bubba stood about five feet six inches tall and carried most of his 180 pounds in his stomach. At first glance, he did not look much of a threat and seemed an easy win for any opponent, but it was a different story when the whistle blew.

Though sloppy in his style and technique, he made up for it with intensity and aggressiveness. He was relentless and pursued his opponents like a lion pouncing on its prey. He had a very explosive and angry personality and was constantly embroiled in fights, irrespective of whether it was an opponent or a teammate. The rage he had when he wrestled made him a difficult athlete to coach.

He was the only student I was actually afraid of, although I never revealed that fear. He was volatile, and I never knew when he would fly off the handle. I believed he would have kicked my butt if he had the chance.

He verbally abused the coaching staff, left training early, and went to blows with any wrestler in the room who crossed him. Ultimately, Bubba wanted to do what Bubba wanted to do. He threatened to quit the team several times throughout the first season, but for some reason he kept returning. I could see he was battling his own demons. Maybe deep down inside of him he knew wrestling was what was best for him. He tried to do what was right, but his anger always seemed to get the best of him.

He was disqualified several times during wrestling matches for biting, head butting, and generally fighting, and, on one occasion, dancing. I recall an actual match when he head butted his opponent and was then warned with a point going in his challenger's favor. He was not perturbed, following with a second head butt, and was called for unsportsmanlike conduct with another point being given to his competitor, and a team point deducted from the Saints.

As the referee blew the whistle to restart the match after the penalty, Bubba started dancing the Chubby Checker twist and then swung his fist at his opponent. It was amusing to watch him shake it on the mat in that instant, but the consequences of his behavior were not too funny. He was immediately disqualified from the match for flagrant misconduct, the Saints lost that match, and the opposing team was awarded six points for the disqualification.

Bubba was also suspended from wrestling in the next competition. On another occasion, he was wrestling the defending California state champion, a young man who was built like the Hulk and technically much better than Bubba. He was an opponent who intimidated all those who stepped on the mat with him but not Bubba. It did not take long for the state champion to manhandle Bubba and pin him, winning the round. As they walked back to the center of the mat, Bubba cold cocked a blow to the side of the champion's head. He staggered to the ground for a moment, giving our team enough time to clear the bench and restrain Bubba while his opponent's coaches did the same as the state champion regained his composure and wanted to defend himself. Bubba's actions reflected negatively, and it was an ugly spectacle for the Saints' program.

He was of course disqualified for the remainder of the tournament and once again was suspended from participating in the next competition, which we needed him in. It was against one of our rivals, Anaheim High School, but fortune was on our side, and we pulled off the win without his participation.

Bubba's behavior was unpredictable. I never knew when his anger would get the best of him. Each match he wrestled was like playing Russian roulette. I felt as though I were sitting on pins and needles, worriedly waiting for him to explode and unleash his fury on his opponent. I sat on edge, waiting to intercede and break up any disturbance he might cause.

Many, no doubt, thought that I should have kicked him off the team for causing continuous grief. I thought about it almost every day, but I knew wrestling was all Bubba had and was hoping that somehow the sport could save him or change him.

On another occasion, Bubba and another thug on the team got into a fight with some local gangbangers. They returned to the wrestling room after school, bragging about how they beat the heck out of them. On the back of Bubba's head was a three-inch gash. He was stabbed with a screwdriver but was a tough kid and was unfazed. I was of course shocked.

Outside of his bad boy exterior, there was a part of him I did like. He was a true competitor and always rose to the occasion when the pressure was on him. He would always come through when it was up to him to win a big match, but his lack of discipline continuously created overwhelming problems.

For instance, at a League Championship Showdown with Ocean View High School, he knew what this match meant to the team, yet he lost his self-control by drinking too much milk the night before and was ten pounds overweight on the morning of the meet. He lost the weight, but when we arrived for the match, he was still a quarter pound over the weight class he needed to make and did not have the stamina to lose it. So close, yet so far. We bumped him up a weight to wrestle the team's best athlete. Amazingly, after all the weight loss, Bubba wrestled an incredible match and lost by a point.

As the years passed, Bubba's attitude got a little better, and it seemed that he learned to control his temper. He even went from a very chubby 189 pounds to a trim 145-pound wrestler within a year. His devotion to cutting the weight showed that he was becoming more committed to the sport. I was expecting some good things from Bubba in his senior year, hoping he would finally become the champion I knew he could be with the right training regimen and positive attitude.

Unfortunately, he fell short of that dream his senior year. His ugly demon, anger, made a final appearance in the postseason playoffs. He head butted his opponent in his first match at the CIF Championship and split the wrestler's chin wide open. He was disqualified once again and was unable to participate in the CIF Dual Meet Championship the following week.

Bubba was one of many that did not get what he could have out of the sport. He did graduate from high school and went on to work various minimum-wage jobs, then moved into construction, and it seems to be a good fit for him.

His two younger brothers tried wrestling but eventually quit, even though they had the same tenacity and mental toughness, but their mean streaks got them into trouble and made it difficult for them to stay focused on the sport.

My wish is to motivate, inspire, and encourage all the Bubbas who have been through my program. However, sometimes the Bubbas of wrestling do not want to be saved. Many get sidetracked by drinking and doing drugs. I even had one wrestler take over his brother's drug dealing business when his brother landed himself in jail.

Some will either get into trouble with the law or get their girlfriend pregnant, thus bringing an end to whatever dreams they may have had. They do not allow the sport to transform them into quality young men who will contribute something worthy to society.

They fight against the change wrestling could make, and they soon self-destruct. I have lost count of how many times I have driven by some of my unredeemable ex-wrestlers who were sadly walking down the street looking confused or lost. My heart breaks for them. How come *they* never found their way out of the clutches of the city or chose to change their life for the better? They had the chance, the opportunity, the support, and the means to make it, yet chose not to. Why? I cannot answer. All I can do is forgive them for the grief and pain they caused me during their tenure in my program and pray that the seed I planted will someday come to fruition.

Reflections on Bubba

Bubba was one of many who didn't let the spark of wrestling and God's love redeem him or free him from the bondage of anger during high school. Bubba has value, though his behavior and attitude did not warrant it—in God's eyes, he had worth. I planted the seed, sent him to FCA camp, and even took him to a few Bible studies. Though he didn't buy into the lifestyle change I encouraged, I have to remind myself I planted the seed of Christ and who he is in Bubba's life. Now it is his choice to redeem himself. As they say, you can lead a horse to water, but you can't make him drink. I lead a lot of wrestlers to the Lord—it's their decision of when or if they'll ever drink. I am okay with that.

I recently spoke with Bubba. I bumped into him after a football game. He's older now, calmer, more levelheaded than when he was in high school. After our talk, I was reassured that he is a new man, a better man, and hopefully somehow God and I had a part in that.

CALVARY CHAPEL–THE CHURCH BOYZ

1994-Present

> It's not staying up that counts ... it's when life keeps knocking you down ... and you keep getting up ... that's what counts.
>
> —Rocky Balboa, fictional boxer in Rocky series

Calvary Chapel is a private Christian high school located on the outskirts of Santa Ana. It is surrounded by shiny, mirrored office buildings a few blocks from the posh South Coast Plaza Shopping Mall in Costa Mesa, where white-collar legions are able to afford designer footwear and expensive diamonds with the swipe of a credit card, a much different world than where the Saints reside.

Moreover, Calvary Chapel is a private school that had the best wrestling program in the state of California. Throughout the 1990s, year after year, they were a nationally ranked team with nationally ranked wrestlers—a team with combined losses that can be counted on half a hand. They enjoyed a program "head and shoulders" above the rest. One could say they were the New York Yankees of high school wrestling, unstoppable, unbeatable, a team that rolled over the competition.

What made them such an incredible team? Many coaches laid claim that the team's coach, John Azevedo, two-time NCAA champion out of California State, Bakersfield, was recruiting some of the top wrestlers in the state, a claim that could be warranted since it was a private school. In Southern California, private schools have no prescribed attendance area; therefore, when an athlete enrolls in his choice of a private school, he is automatically eligible to compete for that team, a rule the public schools cannot practice. Accusations of cheating and slanderous remarks from area coaches, wrestlers, and fans smothered the Church Boyz's successes. "They're winning only because they are recruiting all over the state and country," many people said. The stories or rumors were ugly and nasty.

As a coach who is consistently ranked second or third in Orange County behind Calvary, I wanted to buy into the wrestling community's rumors and despise Calvary Chapel. A part of me wanted to jump on the bandwagon of hatred. However, I could not. I got to know John Azevedo, and I found him to be a quality person with a strong relationship with the Lord, a godly man trying to do what every other coach wanted to do—win! In fact, I envied him and believed him when he said, "I do not recruit."

Nevertheless, instead of crying and complaining about the team's so-called "way of winning," I decided to try to beat them. They were the best, and to *be* the best, you have to compete *against* the best. I wondered why so many other coaches did not adhere to the same philosophy. It seemed as though many teams may have known or anticipated a butt-whooping from them—not the Saints.

We began to schedule dual meets with their team—a rivalry yes, but also another way for the team to improve. Calvary set the bar, and it was my job to get this motley team of wrestlers to jump over it.

The first three meetings during the course of three years were like the U.S.A. invading Iraq. Calvary Chapel's team of wrestlers with years of experience, technique, strength, and conditioning were superb, and their method of attack relentless. Contrast them with the Santa Ana team consisting of young, immature, inexperienced wrestlers, some shy, some timid, some not understanding what they are really up against. Our wrestlers were sloppy and unmethodical, like puppy dogs dropped in the water for the first time, struggling to keep their heads above water. It was embarrassing to watch the wrestling matches. We had a few standout wrestlers who won some matches, but it was not enough to keep the score respectable. However, we never gave up, and the wrestlers never complained about our yearly meet with them as they continued to rise to the challenge. It was a good way to measure how competitive Santa Ana was as a team and as athletes.

In 1998, the Saints faced the Church Boyz again, as scheduled. Our team was young, and most were first-time varsity wrestlers. However, they were talented and under good leadership with future national champions Tony Perez and José Leon forging the way.

The exciting part of the dual was the introduction Calvary Chapel put on before a match. To set the stage, the gym is at capacity—standing room only. The wrestlers emerge from a smoke-filled tunnel extending from the locker room, and both opponents for each weight class walk out to the middle of the mat side by side. As they approach the center of the mat, their names are announced while music like "Eye of the Tiger" is being blared in the background. Fans scream, lights flicker, and strobes are flashed throughout the entire gym. It resembles the scene set for WWE's star, the Rock, as he enters the arena.

Add a big movie screen on one side of the gym wall, with a video feed of the wrestlers upon their entrance. It is dark and smoky with one bright lamp hanging from the ceiling, pointed to the center of the mat. On each corner of the mat stands an eight-foot-tall bank of swiveling and turning lights, mounted to metal scaffolding. Below each one is a police siren that sounds when the Church Boyz put an opponent down for the count and get a pin. They entertained further with a popular Christian rapper performance before the meet. It was rather a classy production.

Their technical crew spent the entire day before the match setting up the sound, lights, and special effects. It is a part of the match they took seriously, and without a doubt, the presentation and performance promoted the sport and drew a bigger crowd to the meet.

Though spectacular, it is intimidating for any visiting team. Being around the fans, lights, music, and special effects even made me nervous, and I was not the one wrestling. They were ranked number one in the state while the Saints were not even mentioned in the top twenty.

Our soon-to-be 1998 National Champion Tony Perez, ranked number three in the state, started off the match. He was up against a "phenom" freshman who had been wrestling twice as many years as him. However, I anticipated Tony would not have a problem as he was older, stronger, and, in my opinion, more technically sound. On the other hand, when the whistle blew, it did not take long to realize the freshman would give Tony a good match.

The score went back and forth with each point notched diligently. I began to notice fatigue set into Tony's conditioning. It was extremely unlike him to get tired so early in a match. He inched ahead with only a few seconds left to score and held on for the win-close call. He staggered back to the bench broken, nothing left in him.

I was concerned about his lack of energy then learned later that he had been running most of the day to shed a few pounds, an activity not recommended hours before weigh-ins, but we were fortunate to win that match and get off to a good start.

Nevertheless, things looked better from that point forward. The 112-, 119-, and 125-pound weight classes all won their matches respectively, followed by the 130, 135, 140, and 145 pounders who pulled off wins and upsets. It was an incredible sight to see the score reading Santa Ana twenty-nine, Calvary Chapel zero. The Church Boyz fans were in utter disbelief, while their coaching staff looked across the mat at us with blank stares. With six matches left, one more win would seal the victory, a feat much more difficult than it appeared.

We were getting to the meat of their lineup, their studs, but even if the Saints did not win one more match, all six wrestlers left to compete had to stay off their backs to avoid the pin that is worth six points. It would be tough but still possible. The Saints' 152-pound wrestler stepped on to the mat and got off to great start, scoring immediately. However, he was never in great shape, and it did not take long for him to run out of gas, fall behind, and lose by a decision, giving three points to the opposing team.

Calvary was on the scoreboard, and the momentum of the match started to shift to their advantage. Their fans started chanting the name of each wrestler who was about to compete. Suddenly, one after the other, both Santa Ana wrestlers who stepped on the mat were pinned in a matter of seconds. The police sirens blare, and the crowd got on their feet while Calvary's three remaining wrestlers looked confident and intimidating. The score read Santa Ana twenty-nine, Calvary Chapel fifteen.

There was a chance the Saints could lose, so my next task was how to keep the next three weight classes from getting pinned; I sensed that they were afraid. The final three wrestlers were very young and inexperienced in contrast to Calvary's three who were seniors and quite experienced. At 189 pounds, the Saints managed to avoid getting pinned but succumbed to the next worse score that could happen in a match—a technical fall.

Being beat by a technical fall in a dual match allows the opposing team to score an additional five points—add that to Calvary's already fifteen, and the score reached twenty-nine to twenty, with Santa Ana still in the lead. Calvary needed one pin and a win to tie with the Saints. Anything better would certainly beat us. My dream of beating the defending state champions was fading away faster than the sunset.

Calvary's wrestlers went into the last two matches fired up and ready to go. Their wrestlers' size and strength, compared to the Saints' made it look like a match between David and Goliath, and as a result, the Saints wrestlers were pinned within seconds of the first round, another victory for Calvary, thirty-two, twenty-nine.

I was proud of the Saints' valiant effort and knew that Calvary Chapel wrestling had a newfound respect for us. I gathered the team together, said a prayer thanking the Lord for a great match, and for the heart and persistence each young man bestowed. We shook hands and congratulated them.

I walked out of the gym with my head held a little higher than usual. I was proud of the team. They gave the number-one team in the state of California, and their fans, the scare of their lives. I believed it showed the wrestling community that the Saints were serious about competing and building a program. It proved that we were a contending team. Calvary Chapel went on to win the 1998 State Championships.

In 1999, we did not avoid the Church Boyz. The Saints' team was stronger, with most being varsity athletes returning, thus we had a chance at beating them for the first time. Their squad was young, though quite experienced.

We did our own light show with music before the match, though it was not as extravagant as Calvary's. We did not have the fortune of a technical crew. However, it was the most anticipated dual meet of the season for all concerned, and, once again, the event was a sellout. The dual got off to a great start with our first four weight classes winning big. The Church Boyz won the next three matches, and the fans were on their feet screaming, yelling, and cheering waiting in anticipation. The place was in hysterics.

The Saints won five of the next seven matches. Calvary never got a chance to take a lead, and the score ended with Santa Ana forty-four, Calvary Chapel twenty-five. It was a momentous occasion. After four years of receiving a pummeling by the perennial powerhouse Church Boyz, we finally attained our goal to beat the best. That win ranks in my top three best moments of coaching, the other two being when Tony and José won the high school nationals.

I was stunned. How did my team ever do it? The odds were against the Saints realistically, and it should never have happened. Only a few years ago our program was the pariah of Orange County wrestling—hopeless. It was hard to believe how a group of young men who had no parental support, who came from the streets few would walk down in the middle of the night, and who worked part-time jobs during the season to support their families, beat such a great team—a great team that had everything it needed to be winners.

Calvary definitely had the expertise in Coach John Azevedo and a large following full of support. Every wrestler's parents at each match or tournament were there cheering their son on. They had the finances to travel abroad and compete, in addition, facilities that paled in comparison to that of a NCAA Division I program. The Church Boyz had it all, but we prevailed and finally beat them. How? Is it because a group of high school athletes finally believed in themselves? Could it be that they learned not to let circumstances and disadvantages in life get the best of them?

The sport evidently taught some unlikely young men self-confidence, self-worth, and persistence. They learned that if they wanted anything good in life they had to fight for it. That is why the sport of wrestling is amazing; it builds and instills a great deal of character in young men, and that character helps to overcome obstacles that life will present.

Unfortunately, however, wrestling is an underrated sport

and is due much more credit than it is ever given. If one could understand and see what the sport has done for those who competed on the Santa Ana team, I am sure one would have a newfound respect.

I am proud and inspired by those I have coached and was elated to see them beat the best. However, it was not only that 1999 team who triumphed over Calvary that night in the Saints' gym but all the wrestlers before them who ever trained to try and beat them. They laid the foundation, began the dream, and most came back to teach the younger ones what they would need to do to fulfill that dream. My hat is off to those who have dedicated their lives to a sport that offers nothing at the professional ranks. Well, nothing in comparison to football, basketball, and baseball. Credit for the team's success is owed to all those wrestlers who ever practiced in that wrestling room and gave it their all.

Calvary Chapel continued their winning ways over us the years following our 1999 victory. However, we did have another barnburner of a match in the 2003 season. Unfortunately, I made a coaching error in my attempt to make a strategic move for the win. It did not work. Therefore, it came down to the heavyweight match, "he pins, we win." It was too much pressure on the shoulders of the first-year wrestlers for the triumph. We lost, but it was fun trying. John Azevedo went on to coach at the college ranks, leaving an alumnus behind to coach the perennial power. Since he left, the Church Boyz have fought hard to keep the program intact and the tradition continued. But it's hard to fill shoes of such a great coach like John Azevedo. We continue to dual Calvary Chapel every year and still have fun, exciting, intense matches that keep the crowd on their feet.

They don't have the dual meet strength as they once had, and we have been fortunate to get a few wins over them in the last couple of years. However, they are still producing state champion wrestlers. Although most coaches couldn't wait for their success to dwindle, it is kind of sad for me to see such a great program take a step back. To be honest, they brought several state titles home to Orange County, thus improving the level of competitiveness in Southern California, something that was much needed, especially in a state where there is only one division with more than 750 wrestling schools competing for the top spot. Hopefully, another team will emerge as a wrestling power and bring back the title to the Orange County. It'd be nice if it were the Saints of Santa Ana.

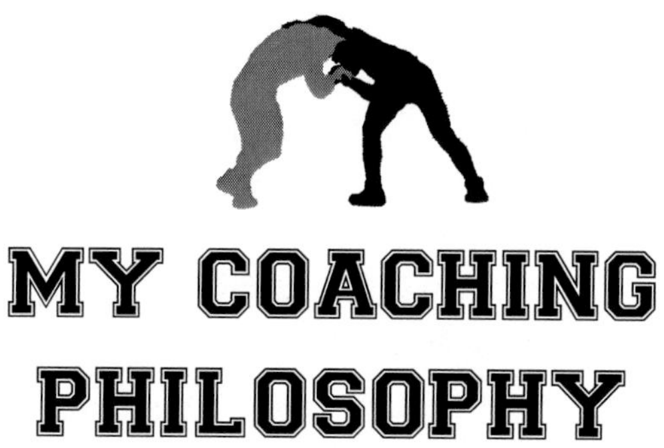

MY COACHING PHILOSOPHY

> We serve others so later others will be served.
>
> —Scott Glabb

As a young coach fresh out of college, I became infatuated with the idea of that first job: that first assignment and opportunity to build a wrestling program and coach a team. It then became a passion. Many young coaches, including myself, place all their value and self-worth into winning. We want to feel important, accepted by our peers. We want our bosses to value us. We want the faculty and staff members to admire us. We place pressure on ourselves to win for our own gratification above that of the team. It simply makes us feel good about our accomplishments and ourselves.

Too often, however, we do not look beyond the job at the core of coaching; that is, to mold and influence in a positive light the lives of young athletes toward a successful future. We must help to build their character, not feed our personal egos by mere wins.

Nevertheless, I was driven to win. But how did I forge these young men into winners? I believe coaches have to be positive role models, and in order to be such, we must follow our own training regimen. In other words, duplicate the rules and upkeep the standards that *we* learned from previous coaches—preceding coaches like my high school coach, Charlie Lemcke.

Coach Lemcke was hardnosed and tough. He often pushed us beyond our limits in training to levels we did not believe possible. Perhaps he was a little too hard on us at times, but he was young, and it was a steep learning curve for him. I, however, looked up to him and modeled his philosophy. I ended up at the same college he attended, so I had the consistency of being under his tutelage following the same coaching model—forceful, unrelenting, and disciplined-based.

When I arrived at Santa Ana High School, I discovered early that the coaching philosophy I so avidly learned was not going to work in this setting. It was impossible to walk into a tough urban school that was dominated by a Hispanic culture that did not place emphasis on sports or imposed discipline. Had I tried to enforce that, there would be no wrestling program.

For instance, basic coaching rules, such as "anyone who misses practice will miss a match" or "any outside actions that will reflect negatively on the school mean you are off the team" or "be on time" and "keep the wrestling room clean and safe" were ignored by my wrestlers. They did the total opposite by skipping practice and matches, and if I exercised authority, they would quit. Therefore, I had to quickly become flexible and work with each student on an individual basis by learning how and where they were brought up and who their parents were. I could not deal with them as a wrestling team. I had to adjust my coaching tactics to meet them in the middle.

I had to be lenient. Most coaches would perhaps consider this too indulgent, but I had a roster to fill up to create a team. If I pushed too hard, there would be no team, and in essence, it was my duty to keep the students *in* sports, not drive them away. I invested time in learning the lifestyles of the students. Many had to work to support large families; some could not walk home from school after hours out of fear, some babysat siblings, some preferred to hang out with peers rather than train. I then set out to find which ones I needed to work with and which ones would be disciplined enough to stay the course. I focused on grooming them without a thought to winning. That would not be an issue once they were prepared.

Soon I realized that my job as a coach was my calling, my purpose in life. Therefore, since it was my purpose, I knew that part of that purpose was to serve my athletes. Sometimes I think coaches fail to remember why they are truly into coaching. They get caught up in the wins and losses and forget that they are there for the kids. We are a selfish society and value our time greatly. Few are called to serve, to give back, to put others before themselves. However, I knew that was what needed to be done to rebuild this program. You could say I lived in that wrestling room. I was the first one there and the last to leave. I never denied helping a wrestler with anything they needed.

Further, I integrated a supportive, personal approach to my coaching style, as I believed being tactile was important to some degree and used affirmations and the proverbial "slaps on the back" to involve contact and build self-esteem. In addition, I encouraged them to share their feelings because I recalled as a teenage athlete myself being rarely asked how I felt about things. I invited the wrestlers to bring their problems and concerns to me without worrying about being ignored or judged. As a result, I learned about their living conditions and their lack of parental support and was able to be there and instill in them hope, which is essential. I impress to all freshmen that they are the future. They are the next Santa Ana High School champions. I point to pictures of past champions on the wrestling wall and tell them that their pictures will be there too. They need to believe that to make it a reality.

The Saint wrestlers were also burdened with the reputation of being vandals and thieves while attending tournaments at other schools. When I first came on board, I heard the unpleasant story about a group of former wrestlers, while competing in a tournament, breaking into the theatre of a hosting school and throwing paint on the walls as well as smashing apart some furniture. Oftentimes, I had coaches tell me that an item had been stolen from one of their wrestlers and ask if I could please investigate to see if one my wrestlers took it. It was an embarrassment to engage in such conversation with coaches. How was I going to change this negative perception about our team among local competitors? I guess it was time to do some character building and try to transform these so-called delinquents into gentlemen. After two-day tournaments, a gym can be quite messy; therefore, when we attended wrestling tournaments I began having our team help the hosting school clean up their gym. We would pick up trash in the bleachers and roll up their mats. The teams who we helped appreciated our efforts and took notice. I also preached to my wrestlers the importance of being a class act and respectful to others at all times, whether it be at a tournament, in the classroom, or at the mall. Before I knew it, the unpleasant complaints and disparaging remarks about our program were being overshadowed by compliments of our well-mannered team. Even today, we still help our opponents clean their gym, and we continue to hear admiring comments about our wrestlers' sportsmanship from coaches, fans, and parents alike.

The most important, however potentially controversial, thing I did to lead these young men to their winning ways was reintroduce them to living a more spiritual life. I say reintroduce because I believe most already had a foundation of Catholicism ingrained into their lives. I took it upon myself to lead them back to what I think they once believed in, God.

I often heard other men and women of God share their stories on how God spoke to them and sent them a message in an audible voice. Yes, I was skeptical—God speaking directly to me? What does he sound like? Is it clear what you hear him say? Well, now I know. God spoke to me in a clear, soft, yet firm voice. It was toward the end of the season of my first year. The team and its athletes took its beatings, and winning was not something any of us saw for the near future. Yet, my young, big ego told me I had to win to be of any worth. So I was persistent to find a way, but it wasn't working. As I stood outside the wrestling room door one late afternoon, watching the guys scatter to go their separate ways after practice, God spoke to me. Some say, "Are you sure it is God? Maybe it is schizophrenia." I don't know how to explain it, but when God speaks to you, you'll know it.

He said, "Give up. Quit trying to win and start investing more time into these kids." That was it, short and to the point. To me that meant I should really share with them who I was by taking them to church and letting them find what I found when I was a teenager. So I did exactly that.

I gave up on trying to win with this group. I decided I would be a mediocre coach with a mediocre program, and in all honesty, I was going to be okay with that. I started a Fellowship of Christian Athletes Bible study after school, and I invited them to church and youth group outings. I figured this was what worked for me and kept me on the straight and narrow. So I spent more time with them and answered their questions about God and who Jesus Christ is. It worked: having faith and listening to God was the answer. The wrestlers bought into it; they really believed if they lived a good lifestyle and got back in touch with God that good things would happen. Within a year's time, the wrestlers who were criminals, the ones who were lost, the ones who lacked talent, and the ones who had no family support, started to turn the corner. They weren't perfect by any means, but they were making the effort. Not only did they start winning, but, more importantly, they became better students and better people. Today I often get caught up in winning and start feeling the pressure to see this team succeed, and then I remember how I got here: faith and trust in the Lord. It is at that moment I give it all back to the Lord and ask him to let his will be done with this program.

My new philosophy and unconventional style of coaching paid off over the years as the success of Santa Ana grew. I was gradually able to reinvest some of the traditional coaching style by introducing the discipline and high expectations that are prerequisites for any sport. With victories come reputation and an understanding by new wrestlers that they are expected to comply, compete, and excel.

Once I gained their interest, I set out to win matches. Success did not come quickly or easily. The first year we won eleven dual meets and lost sixteen, primarily beating teams from similar tough environments. We lost to Marina, the school where I once coached. It was not amusing being beaten by wrestlers I had once coached, but we sucked it up and moved on.

By 1993, Santa Ana won their first league championship, and I felt that I took the program as far as I could single-handedly. I had the talent to develop a consistently successful program, but I needed to be secure enough to invite someone who could add to the program what I could not. It is, without question, essential for any successful program to have experienced and skilled assistant coaches.

Too many head coaches make the mistake of not hiring skilled assistants, perhaps because they want the admiration of peers for their own gratification. Yes, I was apprehensive, fearing an assistant would know more about the sport than I did. With such knowledge and skill, athletes will learn, but the head coach risks losing the respect of the wrestlers. It was certainly a challenge to place my ego aside and employ another voice.

Nevertheless, at a successful Orange County wrestling clinic,

I was fortunate to meet Vince Silva, former Oklahoma State All-American who was coached by two-time Olympic Champion John Smith. He was tremendously impressed with the Santa Ana Saints' tenacity. It was not something he often saw in other wrestlers, and he frequently coached and attended wrestling clinics to lend his expertise, so I handed him the reins, and he took charge of the training sessions. It was a difficult task, but he was an asset to the team.

Vince took the Saints to another level and taught them the style and work ethic that made him one of the country's great collegiate wrestlers. Santa Ana wrestlers began placing in state and winning national titles. Unfortunately for the team, he was offered a job at the college level and left, but we owe him a lot and have retained his regimen and training style.

In 1995, assistant coach Rick Lara joined the team. We were fortunate that he was also a teacher and was based on site at the school. Rick was another person to help me keep an eye on our athletes. He was also an excellent motivator. Further, he had a lot of experience in wrestling, conditioning, and weight training, and he continues to wrestle with the athletes, even though he is well into his forties. He fought hard, giving them everything they could handle. It is an admirable sight. We are proud of him and appreciate his undying love for these young men and his belief in their potential for success, on and off the mat.

During my tenure as coach, I met Joe Gonzalez, a 1984 Olympian, and two-time NCAA champion. He is one of the best-toned wrestlers in history and works well with the athletes one-on-one. Just as important, he was one of few collegiate wrestlers I looked up to when I was young and someone I had hoped to coach alongside.

I hired Joe as an assistant coach a few years after Vince left. At that time, he was looking for a change, wanting to step down from a head coach position to an assistant; my athletic director was able to find him a teaching job in the district. A dream come true, I was working with my idol! Joe brought a wealth of knowledge and expertise to the program, and it was a privilege to have him in our corner.

Santa Ana is privileged to welcome back some of the successful alumni to train with the new wrestlers. Many of them go beyond wrestling and mentor the less fortunate students assisting them outside of school and athletics.

I have learned that one never loses the respect of the team if an accomplished assistant is by his side. The athletes realize that I am not as technically adept as my esteemed assistants, but they know who is in charge of the program, who makes the schedules, who raises the money, who organizes the trips and generally keeps the program alive, and they know the assistants that I bring onboard are a credit to the program. Current and former assistants have enriched the program by sharing their selfless attitude that is essential to helping young athletes. They cared about the students at all levels, not just as wrestlers.

With my new philosophies, my experienced coaching staff, and tenacious group of young wrestlers, the team made an about-face. Winning soon became a habit, an expectation. The tradition of success was now in place. Granted, we have never been the best in the state of California. However, we have achieved more than any of our supporters could have ever predicted.

My experience as a coach at Santa Ana High has taught me that, though the wrestlers may have been at a disadvantage economically, lacked the experience needed to compete with the best, or faced pressure from family members and friends to quit, they still rose above it all to meet my expectations and beat the odds.

Coaches, educators, parents, and athletes could learn a lesson from the past and present wrestlers. Shoot for the best, set the bar high, but have realistic expectations. Never underestimate a kid by thinking, *This kid does not have a chance.* I told myself that several times; I held out no hope for certain wrestlers thinking that they either did not have the talent or the attitude to be a success in the sport. However, they proved me wrong along with several other athletes who tried out for the team.

It is never wise to take too lightly the human spirit. It taught me that no matter how untalented, unintelligent, or unathletic a person might appear to be, he can achieve anything in life as long as he puts forth the effort and believes in himself.

My hope as a coach and educator is to see more people in my profession drawn to work in inner city, urban schools. So many of us have a fairytale picture of working in the best schools and coaching the best teams. We think of how much it will do for our self-esteem if we have successful students and athletes.

I have taught and coached high schools from one end of socio-economic conditions to the other and I can honestly say I have gotten more satisfaction and pride from teaching and coaching those students who were challenged and at a disadvantage than I did from working with those who had it all. To see the miraculous metamorphosis of individuals from the time they entered the ninth grade to the day they graduate and to know I was a part of that change is the most gratifying and remarkable feeling one can have.

STUDENT LETTERS

> Judge your success not only by what you've become, but by what others have become because of you.
>
> —Anonymous

Most people I meet who are not educators think that I am just a wrestling coach. They do not realize that a majority of high school coaches are teachers. If we only coached, we would never survive on the $3,000 stipend they give us for coaching. I went into teaching because I had a passion for the sport of wrestling and wanted to be a coach. That was the next best thing for me since I was not very successful in the collegiate ranks as a wrestler.

What saddens me about being a teacher and coach is that our colleagues hold on to the stereotype that coaches are not very good teachers. We are seen as a group of people that spend our classroom time working on practice plans, scheduling, and the like. Some of us are accused of sitting on our butts reading a newspaper while we give the class busywork. Sadly, in a few cases, it is true.

My passion for teaching is now more important than that of coaching. It may not have been at the beginning of my career, but it certainly is now. The impact one can make in the classroom can last a lifetime, like the impact a coach makes though a coach does invest more time into his athletes than his students. It is just as important to make a difference in the lives of my students as it is my athletes.

The following letters and papers are from athletes I've had on my team and students I have had in my English/speech classes. The last five letters are from coaches and parents who recognized our teams display of sportsmanship and helpfulness. Teachers often complain that they are not paid enough for the efforts put forth in their field. However, each time I receive a letter like one of the following, I realize my real payment is not monetary. My real payment is knowing that I made a difference in a kid's life.

Nothing makes me feel better than to read a letter from one of my athletes or students telling me how God used me to change them. I pray that after you read these letters you too will be inspired to change a young person's life—especially one that sees little hope for the future, or one who can't get motivated enough to turn in any homework. Maybe a kid who is experimenting with drugs or hanging out with the wrong crowd needs *you.* So many of our young people are lost. They need direction, hope, and someone to believe in and care about them.

Hopefully these letters can touch you and draw you to help a young person. And you don't have to be a teacher or coach to do it. You can come from any walk of life. All you have to do is reach out and be a Saint in your city.

A Statement from Ana E.

"Just remember you don't have to be what they want you to be."

Those words have probably been the most life-changing ones I've heard yet. Others may see them as a simple quote with the same degree of meaning, but it changed my way of seeing things. They taught me to accept new and different ideas.

It was during my sophomore year when I had this change. I met the person who has had the most positive influence on me—my English teacher, Mr. Glabb. His class was different from any I have had. He didn't only teach the subject, but he helped us overcome daily obstacles. It was the way he created a different relationship with each student that amazed me the most. He took his job not only as that, but as an opportunity to share his experiences that he knew would help us all understand life a little better and set in a different way every day.

It was his dedication and love for what he did that made me realize so many things. The time and effort he put in his wrestling team and students would leave hardly any time for himself. It was hard for me to understand why he did all of this until he explained it himself. He told me that all of the sacrifices he made for other people and all of the things he wasn't able to do for himself would pay off in the future and do so now. He said that the feeling of satisfaction he gets when he knows he has done something good for somebody else is like no other. This is what makes him go on every day.

After seeing the happiness that is brought when one helps another in any way, my plans changed. Yes, owning a business would bring me enough money to live a good life; and yes, owning a business would make my independent way of things happen. I have learned that monetary compensation will never compare to the satisfaction of knowing one had made a positive change and has helped another in any possible manner.

For everything Mr. Glabb has taught me, I am thankful, for he has made me make necessary changes that will make me happier. I am going to go to college and become a teacher. I want to have the same opportunity to help people in the same way I was helped. People may say that teaching is not a high-paying job, and perhaps this is true. But the treasure I give up on earth, I will receive in heaven. I will do something I enjoy and will be whatever I decide to be.

A Letter from Luz G.

Mr. Scott Glabb
Santa Ana High School

Dear Mr. Glabb,

Thank you for giving me a chance to be part of your class. I truly apologize if I ever made you mad when I made stupid comments about the wrestling program. You are the coolest teacher I've met here at Santa Ana High School.

Thanks for sharing your life stories with us. You are one cool guy, and I hope you remember me and make fun of me when you see me in the halls. Thanks for everything, and I'll come to the wrestling matches to cheer our wrestlers on.

With love,
Luz G.

A Letter from Raul Cardenas

Dear Coach Glabb:

How is this team doing? I started this letter on Tuesday, but today is Wednesday. The mail goes out about every Wednesday at noon, so you won't get this letter until January 3 or 4.

I am no longer at the Marine Corps Recruit Depot, San Diego. This Saturday, we moved up north to Camp Pendleton. Our barracks are pretty much the same. There are about 1,200 recruits on the base at this time. My company has about 300, and the platoon is down to sixty-six. We started with 112.

We are now at the field training battalion. Tomorrow we will shoot our first rounds to zero in our M16 service rifles. We also have our first hike tomorrow. It is only a three-mile hike.

We also get to eat our first MRE. Hopefully our sergeant will allow us to eat that candy that comes in it.

Christmas down here wasn't so cheerful. We didn't even have Mass. We had Mass at night, but not in the morning.

The weird thing is that on Sunday our senior drill instructor allowed the platoon to eat what we received in the mail. A few of the families send us snacks, so we had a very happy Sunday. Though he said no more snacks for now.

We only have five and a half weeks left. The time goes by quickly. I am just going with the flow. I got through the day today; although I can't wait until the day I leave and try not to get ahead of myself. I already told myself that no matter what, I will keep going until I get out of here.

I have learned a lot of things down here. I learned how to fight, how to move fast, how to march and use my rifle. But most importantly, I learned that no matter how tired or how much pain I feel, my body will do what I tell it to do.

I'm missing the civilian world a little. I miss using the head any time I want, eating when I want. I also miss television and video games. I don't know what is going on in the world because there are no newspapers in Camp Pendleton.

The thing that I love is that in five weeks I will be a Marine and not the same old me. I will be a private and will be able to walk down the streets in my Marine Corps uniform.

I still remember the quotes from your English class. I always joked, saying I learned nothing. But I learned a lot. That quote was "He who laughs last laughs hardest." Once I get the final order, "Platoon 2025, you are dismissed," I become a United States Marine. I get to laugh at all the people that just looked at me and said in their minds, "He will never make it."

I also get to thank all of the people who helped me accomplish what has been my lifelong goal. The entire wrestling staff played a huge role. I probably wouldn't even have graduated high school without wrestling. I was all screwed up. Wrestling allowed me to release all my anger legally. Before wrestling, I always had urges to hurt someone. Once I started wrestling, all of that stopped. I would get home tired or have other things on my mind, but wrestling had prepared me for life in boot camp. It's practically taken all of me to get through it.

The first thing I noticed was that I joined the Marine Corps to be in the infantry, But during the last months of high school and wrestling season, my thoughts began to change. I already gave up my plans of joining the infantry. I always thought I had to prove something to people. Wrestling showed me that I didn't. I didn't have to go around trying to show people I was tough. As long as I knew it, it was fine.

I am not afraid of going to infantry. I understand that if I ever have to I can pull the trigger with another human being in my sights. But I don't need to go to war and look for that human being. That much I learned in wrestling. Always being prepared for your opponent was enough. Stuff like that didn't come clear to me until I came here.

I never really talked to anyone because I didn't trust anyone. I always worked faster on my own because nobody else would work in groups with me. Wrestling changed my actions. I started talking more. I also learned to work on a team.

I guess what I'm trying to say is, "Thank you very much." I not only admire you and respect you, but I look up to you. I think, *Here is someone who turned nothing into one of the best teams in the United States.*

I have seen posters that say that coaches or teachers can change one life at a time. Well, this letter is to tell you that from all the seniors that graduated last year you changed my life the most. Every night, you will know that you changed someone's life. My uniform will always remind me that you gave me a second chance to turn my life around, and I took it.

Raul Cardenas
USMC

A Letter from Jesus "Pachex" Pacheco

Mr. Scott Glabb
Santa Ana High School

Dear Mr. Glabb,

I would like to thank you for being such a great coach as well as a friend. The past three years have been an experience of a lifetime.

You have helped everyone, including me, with academic, athletic, personal, and even financial problems. This year is the best year I have had on any sports team. I visited places that I have never visited in my life. Since I have joined wrestling, my whole life has changed completely. While in wrestling, it taught me self-confidence, knowledge of the sport, how to maintain a well-balanced diet, how to work as a family, and how to never give up. The most important thing that I learned was having respect for myself and other people. Treat people like you want to be treated. One thing that you taught me is that if you set your mind on whatever you choose, you will accomplish your goals.

In the near future, I can look back and tell people about my experience in wrestling and how it helped me become a better person as well as a student. Being part of the Santa Ana wrestling team is a privilege, and I feel honored for being a part of it and for having a wonderful coach. Indeed, you are the best coach of any team that I have been a part of in my life. I wish only the best in the future, and once again, thank you for everything.

Sincerely,
Jesus "Pachex" Pacheco

A Letter from Susana Z.

Mr. Scott Glabb
Santa Ana High School

Dear Mr. Glabb,

I am writing you this letter to thank you for being a really good teacher and a really funny person. The first time that I saw you in summer school, I thought that you were really mean, but it was the opposite. "Never judge a book by its cover." I learned that in summer school. I think that you are a very good person and an outgoing teacher. I know that you give everyone a little advice, and that's a really sweet thing about you.

My sophomore year was really fun. I had a lot of fun being in your class. I know that being a teacher and coach for the wrestling team must be really hard, but you know how to make everything work. I also want to thank you for helping me in school and for filling out my recommendation letter. I know that I can count on you.

I wish you the best in life. Stay cool as always, and never give up in life. That's all I wanted to tell you. Say hi to your wife. Thanks again for all of your time in school.

Sincerely,
Susana Z.

An E-mail from Ismael Rodriquez

Hey Coach,

Hey Glabb, this is Ismael Rodriquez, writing to you from across the United States. I am stationed in North Carolina right now. Well, I was just writing to you to let you know that you have been an inspiration to me. From the day I met you in seventh grade until the end of my senior year. I have always had respect for you. Even when I didn't have the grades to wrestle, you were always there. I thank you for that, Coach.

You even helped me find God. Remember, you gave me that book, *The Prayer of Jabez*. Thanks. In about two weeks, I'll be heading to Iraq to start a new journey. They already told us that we are good to go. So hopefully one of these days I'll be writing you from Iraq. I've been keeping up with how the team is doing. Tell them determination is the key! I just remembered the quote you used to tell us, "To be number one, you have to train like number two." Well Glabb, it's been a blast knowing you, you're one in a million. When I come back from Iraq, I'll come by and visit and I'll have a surprise for you. See you in a couple months, most likely a year.

With much respect,
Ismael Rodriquez

A Letter from Freshman Student Lida S.

Mr. Scott Glabb
Santa Ana High School

Dear Mr. Glabb,

Thank you! During the last three months, I have learned many things. You're a fantastic teacher; I think you should be teacher of the year! You make learning fun. Having you as a teacher made me understand that there are many possibilities out there in the world. I really like the stories of your life in high school. Your class is very interesting. Halloween was totally cool when you had that mask on and dressed as Mr. Hummel. The sayings that you put on the board are really empowering. You are a great teacher, and I bid you good luck with everything, and to succeed in your career! So thank you again!

Sincerely, your student,
Lida S.

A Letter from Michael K.

My name is Fester. That's not my given name, but that's what I've been known as. I'm serving a year term in prison. My story may help you, so you might want to listen to what I have to say.

Growing up, I had a normal life. In fact, I like to compare it to the *Brady Bunch*. It all changed one day. My dad was sick. He was going to die. My brother and I did our own thing while Mom spent every day in the hospital with Dad. My brother and I were left with very little choices to survive. No parents. No money. We had shelter, but no food.

The streets offered companionship, money, and things we lacked. So, we joined a gang. There, in the fight for survival, we weren't alone. Drugs became our lifestyle. Violence, our home. Our dad died on October 2, 1993. I was thirteen.

With my dad's death, my mom lost all focus. She started hearing voices and hallucinating. I love my mom, but my homeboys were my family. Drugs, my god. Violence, my religion.

I was arrested for beating someone. That was my first run-in with the law. I was sent to a placement (foster) home. I didn't like it, so I ran away. A week later, I was arrested for trying to stab someone. I was sent back to my first juvenile camp. My brother was also a guest there.

Then, my mother attempted suicide. She was put in a county ward, but was soon released.

When I was released from camp, they sent me to another placement home. Guess what? I didn't quite get by there either, but before I could run, a race riot occurred. They said I caused it, and they sent me back to juvenile hall.

I caught a break. My probation officer at the time did me a favor. I was sent to a small group home in Orange County. It was called Boys' Republic. I actually liked it there. Boys' Republic is a twenty-bed group home. I lived there with nineteen other guys and five staff members. It was an easy program, and we went to public high school—Santa Ana High School.

I was new there, but I was allowed to join the school's wrestling team. That's when I met Coach Glabb. He took special interest in me, and he made me strive to be my best.

Wrestling took determination, commitment, and discipline. I never had these values. We went to our limits, and I learned something. I didn't need a gang. I had a family right there on the mat.

At the end of that season, things weren't so easy. I called an old friend and heard bad news. My mother tried to kill herself again. She opened all the propane valves in her camper and lit a match. By the grace of God, she's survived. She was blown out a window.

I asked the staff at Boys' Republic to let me see her, but they wouldn't let me. So, with tears in my eyes, I packed my things and left. I spent a week with my mom. I also ran into some homeboys. I stayed clean, but the need for drugs was there.

I went back to Boys Republic, but they wanted to remove me. So, I left again.

This time, with no restraints, I went back to my old lifestyle: sex, drugs, violence, and hate. I was "home" again.

I had no money, so I made it the "street way." I sold drugs and robbed people. This gave me a "good" life. Sleeping at homeboys' houses and running amok all day. It was so much "fun." How could I have lived any other way? My gods, sex and drugs, were back to rule.

This life was short-lived though. In May, I was arrested for robbery and assault with a deadly weapon. I was sixteen.

Once again, I was sent to camp—a lockdown community. It is a very controlled environment. We had mandatory exercise, but afterward, we were allowed to play games. One day, we were playing football. I was blocking. There was a recruiter there for a sports camp. After the game, he asked me if I wanted to play high school football. I eagerly agreed.

I was transferred there a week later. Camp Kilpatrick is in Malibu, California. We played football against local schools, yet we were still incarcerated. We only left the camp for football games. My social worker was the athletic director there.

My caseworker was in contact with Coach Glabb. They arranged to have me live with Dave Carbajal, the wrestling team's booster president, when I was released. I was so excited. After four years of either running from the law or being locked up, I was given the opportunity of a lifetime. I was going to live in a house with a great guardian. I was released two weeks before Christmas. I was seventeen.

Mr. C (that's what we called him) and his wife were the best. They gave me freedom, yet discipline. Best of all, I was in a home. Once again, I joined the wrestling team at Santa Ana High School. With his strict discipline at home and order at school, I was under control. I did real well in school. My grades were good.

As for wrestling, there are no words to describe what it meant for me. Wrestling took the place of drugs. I got high on it. Wrestling took the place of some of my love for violence. My anger was released in a controlled, disciplined environment. Coach Glabb taught me restraint and determination. To this day, I don't know why Coach Glabb did so much for me. He loved me when I was unworthy. He taught me when I was arrogant. He showed me how to be the best. When I first walked into that wrestling room, it was to be better than someone else. When I walked out, I was a league champion, part of a championship team. I was a better person. And, I was a man.

Wrestling took the place of all my dangerous vices, except one: sex. I loved women. What else can I say? Only this: sex was my downfall. I begin making phone calls to 900 numbers, making an outrageous phone bill. Mr. C and the coach asked me about it. I lied to them. This is one of the things I regret most in my life. I lied to my coach.

I went to spend Easter weekend with my mother. When I returned, my things were packed, and I was asked to leave. I had nowhere to go. So, that day, I went to work. The whole time, I was trying to figure out what to do. My manager asked what was wrong, and I told him. He offered his home until I found somewhere to live.

I found a room to rent in the area. I was doing well there—working and going to an alternative education high school. My brother was still in the gang, selling drugs and being violent. I loved my brother so much that I had to give him help. He came to live with me.

After about two weeks, my brother started drinking again. I didn't think there was any harm in it, so I did also. Then, I started going to the parties. My gods returned. I started using drugs again.

My life became a circle of using and buying. My sole existence was to get high. I was "home," only in a different city with new surroundings.

I thought that in a new neighborhood, away from my homeboys, I would keep myself under control. It was not to be. My drug habit became too expensive, so I began selling again. I figured I could save some money and spend the rest on more drugs. This didn't last. My money was finished, and I quit my job. Why work? It just got in the way of my party time. Women returned. I had wild parties with drugs and loose women in my rented room. I was soon evicted.

I found another room for rent. I just moved the party. Money became even more of an issue. I could barely make rent. My final vice returned. I started robbing people again. In a new city, with new friends, my life had returned. Sex, drugs, and violence.

One day, I was really strung out and I got into a fight with my brother. Angry, I went back to my homeboys. I was there scarcely two days before I was arrested for robbery and assault with a deadly weapon. This time, the judge wasn't so nice. He gave me seven years in the California Youth Authority.

CYA is a prison for minors. It is a very strict, very controlled environment. And there are a lot of politics. There are rules that must be followed. One rule is that rapists, child molesters, and those who commit crimes against women were not permitted. The penalty, stabbing or death. After being in prison for about a year, a child molester was moved into my cell. I did what was required, and was sent to court with a new case. I plea-bargained to a deal: thirty years in state prison with a minimum of roughly seven years to serve.

While I was in county jail waiting to transfer, the chaplain came to my door. I wasn't a practicing Christian at the time, so I had no idea why he would come. I now wish he never had. My mother had committed suicide.

I've been locked up for almost five years, and I still have about three more. The last time I saw my mother was Easter weekend, that last year. I never felt as much pain as I did at that moment. I could have visited her. I didn't. I could have called her. I didn't. I should have at least been to her funeral. I wasn't. It will be another three years until I can visit her grave.

Why did I love drugs? Why did I love violence? I can't answer those questions. But what I do know is that if I had been sober, things would have been different. If sober, I wouldn't be in prison. If sober, I would have seen my mom, and maybe, just maybe, I could have said good-bye.

Michael K.

A Short Essay by Wrestler Gary Ayon

Friendship

Everybody has friends. They all have different backgrounds, and they all have different stories of how they met. In my life, I've had many friends; however, there's one in particular. He is not like many of my other friends. This person has taught me a lot about life and how to be a better person. My friend is also the head wrestling coach; his name is Scott Glabb. Coach Glabb is forty-two years old and has a wonderful wife and a one-year-old baby. He has been a great help in my life and has also been a great impact in my life.

My freshman year in high school I went to a different school. I had many friends. My day would consist of going to school and hanging out with my friends in the streets. During this time, I had a different point of view in life, thinking I was never going to be a good person. That's the reason I hung around with the wrong crowd. My sophomore year, I moved and attended Santa Ana with the help of my aunt. There, my cousins made me join wrestling, where I met Coach Glabb. At first, he seemed like a nice, funny guy, but I never thought he would have a great impact in my life or become a role model for me.

"People don't care what you know until they know that you care." This is one of the many things he has taught me; in my opinion, this is true. I never cared what he said to me until one day he started talking to me, and then I realized he cared for me. He shared his life with me, and so did I. From this day on, I listened to him because I knew that he cared.

By the end of my four years, I will not only have learned events in history or how to solve equations but also about life. Walking out of high school, I will remember the great memories I had in wrestling, but more importantly, the great friendship I had with Coach Glabb. Every time I can, I will try to come back and help someone like Coach Glabb helped me.

Dear Principal,

I am a parent of a West Linn High School student who is a member of the West Linn Varsity wrestling team. I recently attended the Pacific Coast Wrestling Tournament at Evergreen High School in Washington. Santa Ana's wrestling team participated in that tournament. I was so impressed by the outstanding sportsmanship displayed by all of your wrestlers. They are really a class act. Not only were they tough competitors, but they seemed to be having fun. So many times in sports, competition winning becomes the only focus. You are obviously training young men to be champions in life, not just sports. I was able to use your team as an example to my son of what real sportsmanship looks like. Please pass along this message to your coaches and wrestling team. Congratulations on your second-place finish. Since my son is only a sophomore this year, I look forward to seeing Santa Ana wrestling team next year at the tournament. Keep up the good work,

Pam L.

Hi Coach,

First, I wanted to thank you guys for coming out to our tournament Saturday. I am extremely impressed by your Christian leadership. I wanted to let you know that you opened a wonderful door for me to further witness to our team and parents at La Quinta. The coaches and parents went to dinner after the tournament Saturday, and several of the parents kept commenting (positively) on your team and the large number of Christ-centered shirts your boys were wearing. This opened a wonderful discussion for us. To make a long story short...we now have a mother's prayer group that is going to meet before all of our competitions.

God bless, and keep up the good work,
Tom Jenkins

Coach Glabb,

I am an assistant wrestling coach at Emerald Ridge High School in Puyallup, Washington. I was fortunate enough to witness your wrestling family at the Pacific Coast tournament the past three days. I was extremely impressed by your team. They are obviously well coached; they had great technique, intensity, drive, and poise. What impressed me more was how good of people they are. I always saw outstanding sportsmanship on their part; they won with grace and humility and lost with dignity and respect. Around the gym and high school, they were always well mannered and kind to others. You and your team are doing great things for the sport of wrestling and amazing things for the lives of the people lucky enough to be associated with your wrestling family. I hope to compete with you again.

Good luck with the rest of your season.
Craig F.

To: Administration
From: Wrestling Coach El Toro High School
RE: Santa Ana High School Wrestling Team

I am writing this because it needs to be brought to your attention. Your wrestling team (varsity and junior varsity) was in our ten-way tournament on December 2 and 3. They have been here several years. A wrestling tournament brings together some of the toughest, most aggressive, and sometimes sloppy athletes from many different schools. Because of this, it is difficult to keep the gym, restrooms, and locker area clean and undamaged. Our tournament this year was no exception. It took 2.5 hours to clean the bleachers Friday night!

But there was one area that was clean, both Friday and Saturday. It was the bleachers! I thanked your coach, but that's not enough. Every year he has been here it has been the same.

Not only that, but your wrestlers helped load mats onto a trailer, they helped clean up, and they were respectful through the tournament to me and my staff! And on top of all that, they won the tournament!

I've been coaching since 1972, and this is the first time I have ever taken the time to write a letter of appreciation for something like this.

Again, thank your coach for me, and I hope your team will return again next year.

Sincerely,
Coach Jerry J.

Mr. Dan Salcedo
Santa Ana High School

Dear Mr. Salcedo,

I would like to congratulate you, Mr. Scott Glabb, his staff, and your wrestling team on a job well done. Over the years, we have established a very good and spirited rivalry in the sport of wrestling. We have witnessed some outstanding wrestlers from both of our schools. Coach Glabb and his staff are to be commended for all of their hard work; his teams are always prepared, well coached, and very, very tough. Our coaches appreciate the friendship that this rivalry has brought about. I am not writing this letter to you because of that, however. I wanted to inform you about the unnoticeable things that happened at our match yesterday.

I am writing to tell you about the most amazing thing we have seen in a long, long time. Every wrestler I talked to was the most polite and courteous young man I have addressed lately. Everything they said was said with respect and finished with *sir*. It is very encouraging hearing and something I hope all parents were taking notice of. Just as amazing were the coaches, who lead by example as well as by mouth. At the end of a hard-fought match the coaches and some players went into the stands and started to clean up the debris. That speaks volumes to those who witnessed it. Your fans are knowledgeable and courteous. Even when a match or call did not go their way, they did not boo or get rowdy. They cheered loudly when their player did something exciting or got that needed point or pin.

That, sir, is why I am writing this letter. That is what I think high school athletics is all about. Two teams who fought hard, wrestled hard, and still at the end were able to shake hands and talk to one another in a civil way. I hope other schools are inspired by your example of "Victory with Honor." I hope all saw just what great sportsmanship your team exhibited. Please continue to lead by example. We look forward to our next match, and we want to wish you and your team continued success.

Sincerely,
Mike Rausch, Athletic Director
Calvary Chapel High School

For more info on the Santa Ana Wrestling team, please check out www.sawrestling.com.

If your team, church, or community group would like to schedule an appearance, please contact me at sglabb@yahoo.com.

ABOUT THE AUTHOR

Scott Glabb grew up in the state of Washington. He graduated in 1980 from Evergreen High School in Vancouver, Washington. Thereafter, he attended Pacific University in Forest Grove, Oregon, and took up wrestling for two seasons. He then transferred to Eastern Washington University in Cheney, Washington, where he wrestled two years and coached one season. He graduated in 1985 with a bachelor's degree in speech communication and education. He also holds a master's degree in athletic administration from Concordia University.

In the fall of 1990, he took his teaching and coaching skills to Santa Ana High School at a time when the sport was struggling dismally to gain the respect of the Orange County Wrestling community. In 1993 he guided the Saints to their first league championship then to a further sixteen straight league titles. Glabb's teams have also won eleven CIF (California Interscholastic Federation) titles.

He has, to date, compiled an overall record of 312 wins and 56 losses. He coached 23 individual CIF champions, 48 state qualifiers, and 15 state place winners. Aside from these accomplishments, he is extremely proud of two national championship wrestlers he has coached, Tony Perez (1998) and José Leon (1999). He was awarded the National Wrestling Coaches Association California State Wrestling Coach of the Year in 1999 and was also the recipient of the California Coaches Association State Wrestling Coach of the Year Award for the 2006–2007 season.

He is also involved with the campus ministry Fellowship of Christian Athletes and was honored as the FCA "John Wooden" Southern California Coach of the Year in 2003. Glabb has been married to his wife, Andrea, since November 2000. She is a science teacher at Loara High School in Anaheim. They have two sons and live in Costa Mesa. He is currently teaching freshman English.

The words he lives by: "People don't care what you know until they know that you care."